PIT STOP IN THE PARIS OF AFRICA

Also by JULIE R. DARGIS

Seven Sonnets

PIT STOP IN THE PARIS OF AFRICA

Julie R. Dargis

INDIE HOUSE PRESS

Library of Congress Control Number: 2012913501

ISBN-10: 147764475X
ISBN-13: 978-1-47764-475-1

Published by Indie House Press through CreateSpace.com
Indie House Press
Professional Resources for the Independent Voice
Minneapolis, Minnesota
www.IndieHousePress.org

For my mother

I can tell you all I know, the where to go, the what to do;
You can try to run, but you can't hide from what's inside of you.

—STEELY DAN

*Roadblocks are only temporary hurdles
if you know how to punch out a car...*

—*ANONYMOUS*

CONTENTS

ACKNOWLEDGMENTS

My mother was extremely generous with me as I worked to complete this book. When I discussed difficult and painful issues with her, she listened. She took the time that she needed to reflect. We became closer. I asked her how she felt about some of the stories that I had written about my childhood. She told me that she wanted me to write what I felt was important to tell the story that I needed to tell. For this, I am eternally grateful. My father read the first draft. Thanks Pop, for being my first reader. To my seven siblings, who always supported me while I was away, even though you had little or no idea what it was that I was doing, thank you. Hopefully, you will now understand. For seeing and touching a poet's heavy heart, thank you, Brock, for asking me to write that first sonnet. Thank you, Donna Gross, for fueling me with the confidence to expand the prose. To Jules Hermes, I extend my gratitude for your help in identifying the true beginnings of my story. Trusted readers of the first draft also included my brother, T.W. Dargis, Lisa Lasky, Ralph Overholt, and André Sardo Infirri. Thank you, Lisa, for agreeing to read it again. Many thanks also to Tina Thuermer and Brian Lambert for providing me with professional encouragement when I needed it most. It truly takes a village—a number of friends and colleagues graciously agreed to review specific chapters. Thank you so much, Catherine Bachy, Leslie Cook, Peg Giffels, Jude Grunwald, Cheryl Hessing, Senada Kahriman, Patty McIlreavy, Katie Mohawk, Vanja Paradinovic-Robinson, Cathrine Peterson, Terri Siguenza, Kitty Thuermer, Mike Tidwell, Phillip

Trobaugh, Giorgio Trombatore, and my dear sister, Qs, (Susan Vorderbruggen), for your suggestions and clarifications, all of which were greatly appreciated. I bear sole responsibility, however, for any errors herein. Many thanks to Kathleen Dargis, Michael Gregory, and Jerrod Sumner for your creative support on the cover design. To the many friends and colleagues noted in these pages, thank you for allowing me to use your names— each of you have been an important part of my life. Thank you, Paul, for allowing me to use your photo. Thank you also, for so much more. And to all of my readers, thank you for your interest in my story. My wish for you is that someday you will recount yours. In memoriam—thank you, Friedl Van den Bossche, for listening as I read you my sonnets each day. I miss you dearly, as do many others, including your two beautiful daughters. Thank you for ordering the roasted elephant garlic that night, Tom. It made for a good story. Finally, to the others in these chapters who each touched me deeply before they were taken from this world—I love you and miss you *too much*.

INTRODUCTION

The third time that I landed back in Minneapolis I decided to publish the sonnets I had written while traveling the world over many years. Throughout my travels, my heart crossed many borders. Through poetry, I was able to express the tragedy, heartache, love, and loss that I otherwise held too closely to my chest.

Since I began writing poetry, I have written over forty sonnets in eight countries, although I have lived and worked in many more. In this book, I framed the sonnets and other poetry in memoir, describing where I was and what I was doing when I wrote the poems. To capture my favorite stories from periods in my life when I was not writing poetry, I included additional prose.

Throughout my travels, I met and worked with many incredible people. In these chapters, I include stories and poems about the time that I spent with many of them. Some depictions of my experiences are humorous, others traumatic. Even so, all of my experiences have been beneficial to me in one way or another.

Many people think that I am still in the Peace Corps, even though I returned from Morocco over twenty-five years ago. After I finished my Peace Corps service, I continued kicking around the world in search of adventure. But ultimately, I was traveling the world in search of myself. Following, is what I found.

Julie R. Dargis
Minneapolis
August 30, 2012

Chapter One

IN THE BEGINNING

Minneapolis 1967–71

When I was a child, I had two recurring dreams. In one dream, I peered out the window each night as an army marched down the street outside of my childhood home. After changing my religion without my parent's consent, I began to have a second recurring dream. I was eight years old when I learned—as a newly converted Jehovah's Witness—that the world was going to come to an end.

I was taught in my friend's backyard that the end of the world would not be like any other natural disaster known to man. It would not be an earthquake, or massive rains, or a tsunami that ended the world. The cause was yet to be realized. My young mind struggled to make sense of my newfound faith. Black dots appeared in my dream each night, consuming the world's oxygen as the air we breathed began to disappear.

I was taught that only Jehovah's Witnesses would rise up from the earth when the world came to an end. But this I did not believe. There were many types of people in the world, many religions, and I was intrigued by them all.

As I continued my summertime studies, I sat alone in the sandbox at the head of my friend's driveway—sometimes for hours—waiting for her to wake up and come outside. On my way to her house each day, I skirted laundry hanging between steel poles along the boundary lines of five houses as I took in the quiet, morning light. I treasured the few hours each day that I was able to release the weight of my responsibilities. As I ran through the backyards, pummeling through the space in front of me, a houseful of young siblings and their needs trailed behind.

With the onset of the new school year, I was greeted by my first calling—I became the mouthpiece for the separation between church and state at my elementary school. Speaking on behalf of my friend and myself, I happily assumed the role of gatekeeper of our newly shared faith. Each morning, as the other students stood with their hands to their hearts, reciting the *Pledge of Allegiance*, my friend and I remained seated. "Pledging the flag is against our religion," I offered-up to anyone who had looked at us confusedly during the recitation.

If a song was introduced in music class that was not allowed, I would raise my hand from the bleachers. Standing proudly next to my friend, I announced to the music teacher, "Excuse me, but singing patriotic songs is against our religion."

Halloween arrived. With the holiday came the first class celebration of the school year. My friend's mother came to the school before the start of the party to remove her daughter from the class—nothing was to be celebrated above Jehovah. The party started, but I remained. My teacher invited me out into the hall.

"Why hasn't your mother come to pick you up?" she asked.

As I looked up at her, my eyes passed her gaze and settled onto the geometric swirl that wisped along the top of her brow. "I dunno," I said.

When I returned home from school that day, my mother met me at the door. But instead of a warm hello, I was greeted with an outstretched hand pointing toward the bench at the far side of the enclosed patio. "Go over and sit there until your father comes home," my mother instructed.

I waited until my parents came into the patio to talk to me. As my father stood quietly behind her, my mother kneeled down in front of me.

"Why?" she asked, drawing out her only word. It hung heavily in the air between us. I stared back at her. Curiosity had led me to explore my friend's religion. Studying something new had both opened my mind and set me apart. My new religion afforded me the attention that I desperately sought. I was too young, however, to understand or explain all of this to my parents. Instead, I nodded when my mother asked me to relinquish it.

Returning to the Catholic Church of my youth, I was ten years old when I learned that cows roamed unfettered in the streets of India. It was a Sunday morning and I was sitting in mass. Gripping the corners of the wooden pew, as the priest spoke I sat up and leaned forward. The Sunday sermons often told of those less fortunate. Piety promised a place in heaven. The church expected one to live a life of self-sacrifice. But I was also drawn to the novelty and excitement of cultures other than my own.

When I look back at my life, this is the age when I knew that I was destined to travel the world. I needed to go to India, or anywhere else in the world where life was different. I yearned for adventure. I wanted to see the world for myself. But my early travels would not take me across borders into foreign lands. Six miles would be the first marker separating me from my family and my troubles.

My mother came into my bedroom with my father. I had been hitchhiking with my best friend near our home the day before. My mother had seen my friend on the road, but she had not seen me. In disbelief, I gave myself up. But my honesty had backfired. My mother had decided to send me away.

I was in shock, although I knew that I had an ally in my father. I pleaded with him not to let my mother send me away. I had known young people who had been sent away to be rehabilitated at halfway houses—they were the wild kids. I was not. I had high hopes, big dreams. My earliest report card had confirmed my potential; I was *industrious*.

My father took up the issue with my mother, winning out over her. For days afterward, my mother did not speak to me. The penetrating silence behind her dark eyes cut into me. I needed to find somewhere else to live. I called my best friend to make a plan. We agreed to collect canned goods and frozen dinners from our pantries and freezers. We settled on a place where I could go.

The following day, my friend accompanied me to the home of her friend's grandmother. We packed the frozen food on top of the canned goods, walked to the main boulevard, and stuck out our thumbs. Almost immediately, two young boys pulled over in a jacked-up Chevy. The front door opened, and the boy on the right side of the car leaned forward, pulling his seat forward with him. Loud music pumped out of the back window. My friend and I climbed through the smoke into the backseat of the car, pulling the bag of groceries in after us. The wheels squealed hard against the pavement—I was on my way.

Without knocking, my friend entered the house. I pulled the bag of groceries up three cement steps after her. Young people sat in the living room, spilling out into the kitchen, smoking cigarettes and drinking beer out of bottles. Without the slightest question, the dark-haired woman who lived in the house gathered a handful of snaps on the front of her floral housedress. Pulling the snaps tightly to her chest, she turned and walked into the kitchen. I followed her, depositing my bag of groceries on the floor next to the kitchen table.

As the woman ushered me into the bedroom off of the kitchen, a teenage boy sitting at the kitchen table slipped a lit cigarette between his lips. Slapping his feet onto the ground, he reached for the bag sitting next to him on the floor. He peered into it. Unimpressed, he put his feet back up on the chair under the table in front of him.

Turning from the doorway of the bedroom, the woman reached across the room and planted her index finger into the boy's shoulder blade. "Hey!" he yelped, turning around to see who had poked him.

The woman pointed at the refrigerator across the room, instructing him to put away the groceries. The boy pushed himself up and grabbed the top of the bag, yanking at it lazily as he dragged it across the linoleum floor.

Standing under the frame of the bedroom door, I looked over at the woman's daughter. She pulled a brush through her long, black hair as she sat gazing at me through the mirror in front of her.

My friend came into the kitchen to say good-bye. It was a school night for her, she needed to return home. Crossing the street in front of the house, she turned and put out her thumb. As I watched through the front window, a car stopped and she hopped in.

A small, portable, black-and-white television was turned on in the corner of the living room. The grainy picture was silent. I slipped into the corner of the couch, but the smoke in the room stung my eyes. After a few minutes, I returned to the kitchen, where I sat on a chair that had been pushed up against the wall, dangling my arms loosely between my legs. I stood up and went into the side bedroom. It was empty. Exhausted and alone, I fell onto the cot that had been pulled out for my stay.

The next day, my mother pulled our family car into the driveway in front of the house. My friend had not told my parents where I was when they had asked her as she stood waiting for the bus that morning. And for this, my mother would never forgive her. Once home, I had been freed of blame. Yet, it had been my friend who had seen the anguish on the face of my father that morning. As soon as she had arrived at school, she had gone to see the guidance counselor to confess.

The guidance counselor notified my parents, but not before the police had arrived to begin an investigation for a missing child, posing questions that would haunt my mother for years afterward.

As the engine hummed, my mother stepped out of the car. I stood in the front doorway. When my mother saw me, she called out to me, instructing me to get into the car. I don't remember thanking the woman in whose house I had stayed. I don't remember saying good-bye. I simply climbed into the car, leaving the canned goods and frozen food behind.

As an adult, when I see girls the same age that I was when I ran away, it stuns me when I realize how young I was. With time, I came to understand my mother's motives for wanting to send me away. She was doing her best as a parent, no doubt. Her methods, however, were clouded by the past. Recalling painful experiences from her childhood, she relived these experiences through my life.

My mother had been sent away as a young child. After being widowed, my grandmother returned with my mother and her brother to the small, crowded house of her extended, immigrant family. When my mother was four years old, my grandmother became engaged. Because she was working full time—unlike other women of her generation—the parents of my grandmother's fiancé offered to take my mother in.

My mother was well cared for in her new home. She was the center of attention, something that she had not experienced in her own family. Within a few months, however, my grandmother's fiancé contracted tuberculosis and died. Even so, the family of the deceased man wanted my mother to continue to live with them. They offered to adopt her, but my grandmother would not allow it.

Some years later, a second marriage took my grandmother to California. My mother was left behind, once again separated from her mother. Twice as a young adult, my mother traveled to California to live with her mother, but after a year or two, my mother returned to Minneapolis where she lived with her aunt and her grandparents.

Many years later, my mother would sit with me and recount the experiences in her life that had left her feeling abandoned and alone. A day would come when we would talk about our lives as friends. But when I was a child, we did not discuss issues such as these. Rather, I, too, learned to steel myself, when left to my own devices.

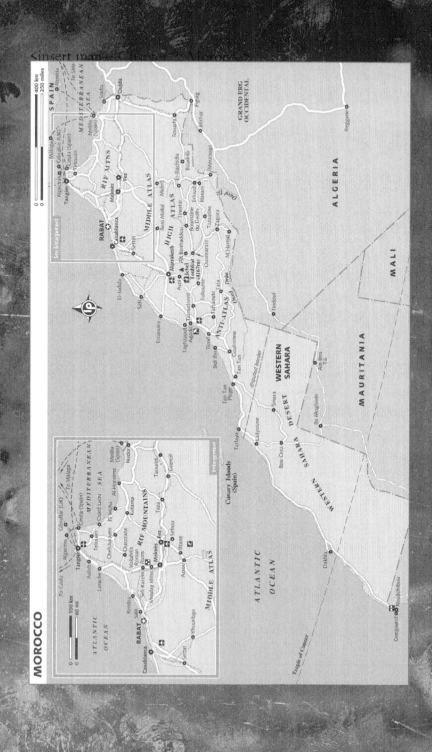

<insert image: Chapter 3 – Morocco>

Chapter Two

THE PEACE CORPS YEARS

Taroudant 1984–87

They passed in single file. The boys left first, shaking my hand with rigorous enthusiasm before placing their hands gently upon their hearts. The girls waited quietly until all of the boys had left before proceeding to say their good-byes, smothering my face on both sides with kisses. A particularly hardworking student approached. A tear had surfaced upon her face. As she kissed my cheeks, a flood of memories flashed through my mind. Her work had always been the brightest, but it was her emotions that set her apart.

The last day of school was the most memorable day of my Peace Corps experience. As I walked home I was exhilarated. Images rushed through my mind, but there was only enough room for two words—two years. From the day I had arrived I could feel their stares about me. The students had watched me, and tested me, and finally—after two long years—they were showing me that they cared.

The day I left for Morocco, my three youngest siblings were setting off on a road trip with my parents to California. It was an early morning in June 1984 when my parents dropped me off at the airport on their way out of town. It would take my family three days to arrive at their destination. I was flying to Philadelphia, to spend three days at a pre-departure orientation before continuing on to Morocco, where I would stay—without going home—for two years.

We settled into a lounge area next to the departure gate. My mother's hair was black, my father's light gray. My three youngest siblings were teens. Two sisters, no longer living at home, two childhood friends, one college friend, and a hung over colleague joined my family to see me off.

I looked up at the clock. The gate attendant asked all passengers to board. I waited until all of the other passengers had passed through the gate before I walked down the incline toward the Jet way. My family and friends lined up along the railing. My mother began to cry. Everyone was waving and yelping good-byes. Tears were in almost all of their eyes.

At the departure gate, I turned and looked up the incline. My young nephew was standing at the top. "Good-bye, Auntie Julie, I'm gonna miss you!" he yelled at the top of his lungs, over and over.

I handed the gate agent my boarding pass.

"I don't know what all the fuss is about," I said. "I'm only going to Chicago for the weekend."

A burst of laughter shot down toward the departure gate. I stood for a moment, savoring the string of smiling faces. I pulled out my camera, took a photo, and waved good-bye. Hooking the straps of my carry-on bag over my shoulder, I turned, passed through the boarding gate, and stepped onto the Jet way.

Although I had the advantage of teaching my native language as a Peace Corps volunteer, it was a challenge to create a learning environment that was relevant to the students. I studied as much as I could about the culture, weaving aspects of the students' daily lives into lesson plans. My students traveled from class to class as a unit, moving together from teacher to teacher throughout the day.

One day after school, as I passed the science department, an attractive, dark-haired science teacher stood hovering in the doorway. I continued to the front gates. Outside the school grounds, the young teacher slipped into step next to me as I walked home. We talked of our students. We both taught the tenth class of the seventh level—the wild students who had been clustered together. He invited me to coffee.

I was the only woman in the coffee shop. We sat in a back corner, away from the street. He was from Marrakech. His family owned a small photo shop in *Jamaa el-Fnaa*, the central square known for its large market—the narrow, winding streets and back alleys an impossible labyrinth to navigate unless you had grown up or lived there.

He had been assigned to Taroudant by the Ministry of Education after obtaining his teaching license. He lived with three other male teachers who had been assigned there from other parts of the country. They shared an apartment inside of the ramparts, which had been built to enclose the small city in the fourth century. Ahmed was surprised to learn that I also lived within the walls of Taroudant. All of the other expatriates lived in villas on the outskirts of the city.

"I'm with the Peace Corps," I said. "I'm paid a stipend every month similar to your salary."

He didn't believe me.

After leaving the initial training program, I had traveled on public transportation to reach my site. I had arrived in Taroudant alone, after a twelve-hour overnight bus ride from the capital. During training, I had met a second-year volunteer who had taught in Taroudant the year before. She had given me the name of a man who owned a café along the central ring road. It was the only contact that I had had when I arrived in the wee hours in the morning, two months earlier. Sitting with Ahmed, it was the second time that I had been in the café.

The owner, a small man, came over to our table. He greeted me in Arabic. After shaking my hand, he placed his hand gently upon his heart—a mannerism that I would adopt and use for the rest of my life.

"How are you? How is your family? How is your mother? How is your father? Well? How is the other American teacher, your classes, your friends? All well?" he asked.

I returned the greeting, asking a string of questions, punctuating each with, *lebes,* well, and *kulshi lebes,* all well. Although I could not speak Arabic, I was able to greet Moroccans for three minutes or more at a time, without making a mistake. But my language abilities quickly ended once I had ascertained that all was well.

In time, I would also learn a smattering of the local Berber dialect. The Berbers were indigenous to Morocco, having inhabited the mountainsides for centuries. The area of present-day Morocco was under Byzantine rule until 682, when the Arabs invaded Morocco, converting the indigenous populations to Islam. The Berbers maintained the core elements of their customs and language as the Muslim religion and Arabic language enveloped the national culture.

As in any culture, local populations appreciate any attempts that foreigners make to learn the local language. Many of my neighbors were of Berber descent. They spoke *Shilhah*, the most southerly of the three Berber dialects spoken in the country. Over mint tea and warm bread dipped in argon oil, I learned to count to ten in *Shilhah*. I was taught a popular proverb: *Imic simic asickshem arrhem teakint*, little by little the camel goes into the cous cous pot.

If I found myself in a Berber's home, before the tea was poured the same question was offered: "Do you speak *Shilhah?*"

This was my cue to sit up. "Oh, yes," I said.

I then proudly proceeded to count to ten, forgetting or fumbling at least four of the numbers. Laughter, tears, my hosts began rolling on the floor. I recited the proverb. Wide-eyed, hands held out in front of them, "Stop, stop," they cried. More laughter, they could endure no more. It was the first time that they had ever heard a *Nazarani*, a non-Muslim, speak their language. Tea was poured, and conversation resumed, in broken English.

I ordered a *café cassé*, a small glass of hot milk with a shot of espresso. Ahmed was impressed. I told him that I had studied language for three months with a group of American teachers in Kenitra, a city in the north of the country prior to coming to Taroudant. He asked if we could meet again. He wanted to practice his English. I agreed.

A week earlier, while walking through the circular street in the interior of the walled city, I had spotted the male cousin of my neighbor. We had both been at my neighbor's house earlier that day, drinking mint tea with the family in the courtyard. But when he saw me on the street, he ignored me. Within minutes, another young man whom I had never met came up to me on the street, rudely engaging me in conversation as he walked next to me uninvited. The next time I visited my neighbor, I asked if I had done something to offend her cousin.

"No, no," she said. "He was respecting you."

"Oh," I said, not entirely sure I understood what she had meant.

I had a site-mate in Taroudant, another female volunteer. During our initial three-month pre-service training program we were sent to visit a second-year volunteer in a coastal town. We had sat next to each other in the center seats of the plane while traveling to Morocco. But we had spoken little to each other on the flight. During our first site visit, however, we traveled well together—eating, napping, and rising in sync. Over the summer we became friends, traveling throughout the country with a French teacher we had met on our first site visit.

At the end of the training program, the list of potential sites was posted on the wall. We were allowed to submit up to three preferred sites. The new volunteers vied for the coveted sites where the students were known to be more manageable, or where they had met new friends or lovers. Some volunteers wanted to live in the mountains. Others close to Europe, the desert, or the sea. A few volunteers had given the Peace Corps staff an ultimatum—if they could not go to the site at the top of their list of choices, they would go home.

During the pre-service training program, a number of volunteers had been sent home for reasons of illness or lack of technical ability. Some volunteers had chosen the Peace Corps for the wrong reasons. For months, after arriving at their new sites, volunteers chose to go home. For those who stayed, friendships were cemented that would last a lifetime.

Sarah and I had both noted that we would go wherever we were needed. When we had applied to the Peace Corps, we had both said that we would go anywhere in the world. The week before being placed in our sites was not the time to change that commitment. We were both sent to Taroudant, one of the nicest sites on the list.

In Taroudant, we talked for hours about our students and ideas for lesson plans. We had arrived and found living accommodations separately. But, the culture threw us together during our second year as we quieted the constant barrage of questions from our Moroccan friends and neighbors, who could not understand why a woman would even consider living alone.

The week after I had coffee with Ahmed, I met with him in the science lab at the school. We discussed the lessons that he was teaching his students. They were studying electricity— the three effects of current. I worked with him to translate key French vocabulary into English. I wrote a reading exercise for my students, incorporating elements of their science studies into their English lesson. The next day, my students answered the comprehension questions easily, using their new vocabulary in English to reinforce the concepts that they were studying in their science class. One of the students shot up his hand.

"Miss, you sure are smart," he said.

"I had a good teacher," I replied.

"Give us a song!" collective voices sang out.

The students wanted to learn English through pop music. I worked with a volunteer in a neighboring town to create a visual aid to teach the song "Thriller," by Michael Jackson. The song was fifteen minutes long. I worked on the vocabulary with the students to prepare the class for the listening comprehension for three days.

After they had listened to the song twice, I asked the class, "What is a thriller?"

Hands shot up. I called on a student.

"A horror movie," he said.

At a regional meeting a few weeks later, my fellow volunteers would not share in my victory. They could not believe that it was possible to teach such a long, complicated song.

"But, Julie," said a fellow volunteer, chiding me, "how did you teach *funk?*"

A second-year volunteer from a neighboring town arrived for a visit. I had been in Taroudant for two months and my Arabic language was still minimal. During training we had received three months of technical, cultural, and language training. Early on, I was placed in a group that was to become the most proficient in Arabic. After a week, I was sent to a lower level.

At the end of our pre-service training, we were tested for Arabic proficiency using the State Department rating scale of zero to five. Most volunteers hovered around a rating of two. I was given a zero+, the lowest rating for the group.

"You have absolutely no grammar and very limited vocabulary," the tester had told me after the oral exam. "But you can communicate, so I'm going to pass you."

I had answered most of his questions with my hands.

I walked with the second-year volunteer to the local *hanute,* to buy provisions for lunch. I went to the small grocery store to buy fresh bread, butter, Coca-Cola, and yogurt every day on my way home from school. I ordered the items in Arabic. I paid the shopkeeper and turned to leave. In a bid to impress the second-year volunteer, I twisted my body toward the shopkeeper and thrust the large bottle of Coca-Cola into the air.

"Hawi minbad, In'sha'allah!" I said.

Three old men sitting on large bags on rice against the wall inside of the shop grabbed their turbans in unison, laughing as they mimicked the phrase. I smiled broadly, proud of my proficiency.

"Whaha, leila, li briti," As you wish, miss, the shopkeeper said.

As soon as we were out of earshot, the second-year volunteer looked over at me.

"Do you know what you just said?" he asked.

"Yeah," I replied. "I told him that I would bring back the empty bottle later. He's so nice. He never makes me pay the deposit."

"Did you know that there are three 'h' sounds in Arabic?" he asked.

I looked back at him, hoping to be tutored. Second-year volunteers often mentored newly arrived volunteers, translating words, teaching vocabulary, and providing grammar tips. He spit out three sounds. The first sound emanated from the back of his throat.

"You used the wrong one," he explained.

"Oh, then what did I say?" I asked.

"You just told him that you would have sex with him later."

When I had begun to frequent the store there had not been anyone other than me and the shopkeeper when I made my purchases. As the weeks progressed, there wasn't a day that I had not seen at least three old men sitting against the inside wall of the shop each day that I arrived after school.

"I was wondering why he hadn't invited me to have lunch with his family," I said. "Now I know why."

My apartment was on the third floor of a three-story building located on a small square beside a mosque. There were two small rooms at the far end of the apartment. One housed my mattress; the other was used to pin up a large poster of a caravan crossing the desert that I had purchased in the market. The small, central room was open. Each night, a roof of stars hung overhead. Off to the side of the central area was a squat toilet. Next to the squat toilet a single, brass water spigot reached out of the wall.

The only door was at the top of a long, narrow stairway. An overhang covered a small foyer near the door. A covered kitchen with a large window and a second, single water spigot was located next to the door. The rent, which was paid in local currency out of my monthly stipend, was the equivalent of forty US dollars a month.

From the small, wooden door of the apartment to the bedroom across the open courtyard it was ten paces. On rainy nights, I darted through the open air to reach the rooms on the other side. Off to the side of the central room there was a six-foot rectangle—an opening to the second floor apartment below, where a young married couple, Mustafa and Aziza, lived. Their conversations, and arguments, swirled up through the wide opening each night. But although I heard every word, I understood nothing of what was said.

On the ground floor—the first floor—there was an apprentice shop owned by a little person. Each day, ten young boys crowded into the small space to hand-sew white robes that were sold in bulk before religious holidays. Returning after school each day, I smiled and waved at my neighbor, the tailor. He ignored me. Good, I thought, he respects me.

One day, on a weekend, I slipped down the steps in my nightgown to deposit the garbage bin outside of the front door. The tailor was standing outside of his shop.

"Good morning!" he said in Arabic. "How are you on this beautiful morning?"

I nodded, turned, and quickly mounted the steps to my apartment. He had not spoken to me when I was in Western clothing. But when I was dressed like a Moroccan woman, in a nightgown, he treated me as if I were a sister.

In the evenings, I sat on the tile floor against the wall under the overhang, writing out lesson plans for the next day. Five times a day, beginning before dawn and ending after dusk, the *muezzin* wailed soulfully into a bull-horn attached to the top of the mosque. One rooftop separated my open apartment from the mosque. Each night, as the call to prayer began I put down my pen and closed my eyes as the lyrical cadence of the *muez-zin's* voice poured over me.

A week after I had arrived in Taroudant, I went to the market. I bought a mattress and laid it out on the floor. I bought a few kitchen supplies. I ordered one wicker table and two wicker chairs. When the furniture was finished, I rolled the items home in a borrowed wheelbarrow.

I tacked a poster of Asilah, a northern coastal town and site of the annual arts festival, onto the back of my apartment door. I closed the door and looked around the open room. It was the first time that I had had a place of my own. Later that night, under the stars, I sat on the floor leaning against the wall. Until that day, I had never known how much that I enjoyed the quiet.

When I wasn't spending time with my site-mate, I met with Ahmed. He stopped by my apartment, leaving notes on the door if I wasn't in—raising eyebrows if I was. When we spent time in my apartment, I left the door open, but few people could see up the long, dark stairway. As we sat talking in the open courtyard on the top floor, the continuous chatter through the opening to the apartment below dimmed. As my neighbors practiced their listening skills, Ahmed practiced his spoken English.

I preferred spending time at Ahmed's apartment where we had more privacy. At his place we laughed and joked with his roommates, drank coffee, or watched films. I often stayed the night.

Ahmed organized an evening of activities at the school for the male teachers. He invited me to attend the event with him. I wanted to attend. I knew so many of the younger teachers.

But I also knew that it would cause a scandal. The older, more conservative male teachers would not appreciate my presence. Women did not do such things.

For a time, I believed that I was able to move around town freely, without being noticed. In the evening, I slipped into the entryway along the narrow street of Ahmed's apartment building. In the morning, I rose early on days that I had to teach, so that I could return home before sunrise to shower and dress. But as I walked in the pre-dawn darkness, although I was alone I felt as if hundreds of eyes lay eerily upon me—judging me. I passed under archways that cast dark shadows upon the streets in front of me. As I made my way to the small square where I lived, it was as if the scarlet letter had been sewn upon my chest during the night.

I enjoyed my relationship with Ahmed. We got along well. He was an interesting and engaging friend. He was a sweet and gentle lover. But as time wore on, I struggled with the consequences of being in a romantic relationship in the small town of Taroudant. Spending time with Ahmed was eroding any respect that I had earned with my students, their families, and my neighbors—the one thing that I coveted most in my professional life.

The winter break between semesters was approaching. Over the holiday, I traveled to Spain with three friends. For a short period, I re-entered my Western lifestyle, enjoying cocktails, comfortably sitting in outdoor bars and restaurants, eating spicy pork sausage, and attending mid-night mass on Christmas Eve.

The week before I had departed Taroudant, I had had an early morning class. When I entered the classroom I was welcomed by a large heart that had been drawn on the chalk board by my students. An arrow had been drawn through the heart, pointing at a message below: *You are my sweetheart.*

In a show of disrespect, the students had not waited for me to enter the classroom that morning. I set my bag down and took out my notes. I crossed the classroom and picked up an eraser. I erased the heart and wrote the date at the top of the right hand corner of the chalkboard. Knowing that something had drastically changed, I began the lesson as if nothing had happened.

I considered my options while I was away. I shared my struggles over red wine and chorizo, provisions that my friends and I had bought before climbing onto the overnight train from Seville to Madrid. Prior to departing for Spain, I had decided not to see Ahmed again. Initially, the wine had softened my resolve. But the further I traveled away from Morocco, the more the confusion of my experiences had dissipated. By the following morning, before I arrived in Madrid, I had changed my mind.

Back in Taroudant before the new semester resumed, I went to see Ahmed at his apartment. He had returned, but his roommates told me that he was no longer living with them. I asked them why.

"He is living with his new wife," one of his roommates told me. "He was married to a family friend in Marrakech over the break. They are living in a small villa outside of the walls."

"I didn't know that he was engaged," I said.

"Nor did we," his roommate replied.

It would not be the first time that a young teacher at the school would leave over a school holiday and return with a wife to the surprise of his friends and colleagues. Sometimes he had selected his bride, sometimes he had not. Arranged marriages were common among extended families and longtime friends.

I did not understand how my contemporaries at the school could enter into arranged marriages. In time, however, I saw firsthand how arranged marriages could grow into happy, loving relationships. As in any culture, some marriages in Morocco were not successful, whether they had been arranged or not. Still, my Moroccan friends argued that an arranged marriage was a viable alternative to a love marriage. One Moroccan friend offered me proof in the form of statistics.

"Americans," he said, "have a higher divorce rate than Moroccans. Perhaps you should try an arranged marriage. I have a cousin."

I was not to experience marriage in Morocco, nor was I ever to see Ahmed again. My remaining time in Taroudant was spent honing my teaching skills. Romantic relationships had been relegated outside of the medieval walls.

There had been a draught the year before I arrived in Morocco. Many of my students came from agricultural families and were struggling as a result of the weak harvests. When the rains came, my students rejoiced. They were giddy—their attention could not be coaxed back to the lesson.

"Praise Allah, teacher!" they said. "The rains have come!"

I thought back to the summer storms in Minneapolis. The day my brother was born, the skies were mauve then dark gray. I stood outside waiting for the news. It came quickly. Within twenty minutes of arriving at the hospital, my parents' eighth child—their first son—was born. It was the only time that I had rejoiced after a rainstorm, until I arrived in Morocco.

Once the rains began, they did not stop for five days. Water pulled makeshift houses of thin mud and cement off of their moorings against hills in the countryside. One of my students lost his home as it slid off of the hill in a landslide. I spoke with the other Moroccan teachers, asking them what they were doing to support the student's family. I offered my student the same amount of cash that the other teachers had given him. It was late fall. For months afterward, my student came to class in the same worn *djelleba*. The long, brown robe was the only clothing that he owned.

In the spring, the student who had lost his home during the rainstorm asked to walk me home from school. He had been instructed by his father to give me something to show his gratitude.

"I gave the same amount of cash as all of the other teachers," I said. "I don't need anything in return."

He insisted.

"Teacher, my father said that I must do this. *Minfudlik,* please, may I walk you home from school?"

I agreed.

As we passed the market, my student asked me to wait. The wall of the city was one mile in circumference. Inside of the wall, the central road moved in one direction. I had been uneasy walking along the main road when I had initially arrived in Taroudant. Donkey carts, bicycles, and pedestrians wove in and out of each other as the occasional small, French car nudged its way through the crowds. In time, I observed that there was a method to the madness, and I was able to skirt through the crowds with ease—once I had learned to go with the flow.

My student reappeared from inside the market and we resumed walking. A large, white sack was slung over his shoulder. The bulky sack lay heavily upon his back as he walked. When we reached the square where I lived, he dropped the sack at the steps of my apartment.

"My father asked me to give you these oranges," he said.

I looked at the large bag. It was more than a case. I opened the top of the bag and fished out three oranges. "How kind," I said. "Please thank your father for me."

I turned to go up the stairway.

"No, miss," he said, "my father told me to give you the whole sack."

It was an expensive gift for a family that had recently lost everything. I already had received two cases of oranges from the families of other students earlier that week. My student stood patiently, wedged against the bulging sack of fresh oranges. I looked down at the sack. The gift that I wanted the least was the one that I needed to accept the most.

"Thank you so much," I said. "Thank your father, please, for the generous and kind gift."

My student grinned broadly. It was the first time that I had seen him smile since the rains.

My site-mate and I traveled together on weekends, taking a taxi to the neighboring coastal town less than an hour away, on overnight trips. After paying the equivalent of ten US dollars, we checked into a tourist hotel and took turns using the shower. Neither of us had hot water in our apartments in Taroudant.

We sat on the boardwalk. Lunching over hamburgers and beers, our eyes darted up and down the walkway as we looked out for our students. It was a risk to drink alcohol in the open air. We didn't want to spoil the good reputations that we had built up in our small town. Still, we bought bottles of wine, sneaking them back into our apartments, worried about how we would dispose of the empty bottles in Taroudant once the wine had been drunk.

We were invited to a Peace Corps technical training in the north of the country. To get there, we needed to board an overnight bus at ten at night. The route snaked through the High Atlas Mountains before depositing us in the capital city early the following morning. It would be impossible to sleep as the bus rolled over heavily potholed roads throughout the night. We bought our tickets and boarded the bus. The attendant placed our baggage on the top of the bus and seated us directly behind the conductor. Six hours later, we stopped at a rest stop.

Small braziers glowed in the dark. The warm smell of roasted meat wafted on the mountain air as stars illuminated the space between the hills beyond. The men dispersed into the bushes; the women squatted in groups behind the bus.

"I'm going to find a place that's dark," my site-mate said.

"Do you want a brochette?" I asked.

"Yes," she said. "Thanks."

I walked over to the row of open-air stalls. The hot coals along the string of braziers shone under the skewers of meat. "Two liver brochettes," I said in Arabic.

The vendor pulled a skewer off of the brazier. He placed it between a half-moon of soft French bread, pulling the stick out as he pinched the sides of the bread.

In Morocco, it was usually the male Peace Corps volunteers who lost weight and the women who gained. It was a mystery as to why. I had been ill in training—with amoebas twice and shigella, a more serious parasitic infection, once, uncharacteristically shedding twenty pounds during my first three months in Morocco.

During my pre-service training, I had been transferred to the Peace Corps office, where I had stayed alone in the sick bay for three days. A second-year volunteer, assigned to provide logistics for my group, sat waiting to drive me to the capital.

Vomiting as I reached to open the car door, I walked away and sat against the outside wall of the dormitory. I pulled myself up and went back inside of the building with severe diarrhea. When I returned to the car, I climbed in slowly. Once I was in the front seat, I pulled the door shut and looked over at the attractive, second-year volunteer.

"So, what do you think of me so far?" I asked.

"Do you mind if I smoke?" he replied.

My site-mate found me sitting despondently at a wooden table under the stars, two liver brochette sandwiches lying idly on the table in front of me. She sat down and reached for a brochette. We ate in silence. Traveling without sleep had made me irritable.

"Sarah," I said. "He gave us the penis."

She stared back at me.

"What?" she said. "Shut up, that's gross."

I looked back at her, chewing.

"It's the penis," I said. "I'm sure of it."

"Stop it; just eat," she said.

"Do you want to know how I know that it's the penis?" I asked.

She ignored me.

"I know," I said, "because I just swallowed the tip!"

It was not the first time that we had been surprised by the contents of a meal.

Morocco has some of the most delicious and nutritious cuisine in the world, and Moroccans are extremely generous, sharing meals with guests as a way of life. Being raised by an Italian American mother, I understood this generosity with food. Food was a way to unite families, to express love. In Morocco, hospitality was also an expression of pride.

I was invited to the homes of my students regularly. I coveted these invitations, especially on Fridays when most families served couscous to celebrate the holy day. School closed at noon on Fridays. For hours beforehand the students were abuzz in anticipation of the meal that would be served after the mid-day prayer. Under their breaths they pined for it as the din of *"sooksu, sooksu, sooksu,"* couscous, couscous, couscous, spun off of their lips, propelling them home.

Months later, after returning from the overnight bus trip, Sarah and I were sitting over lunch in the house that we shared during our second year. Our maid, Zubaida, who had worked for a string of Peace Corps volunteers in Taroudant prior to our arrival, had prepared a Moroccan meal for us.

Zubaida worked in our house twice a week, helping us with shopping, meals, and laundry—which she did by hand. I often ran into her on the street. Her long, dark *djelleba*, the robe that covered her body from head to toe, was accented by a lavender veil. The veil was pulled up over her face and attached with decorative pins at the side of her head, under her eyes. The sparkle in her eyes called out to me on the street. I also recognized her shoes. She was a single mother with a twelve-year-old child. She never spoke of her child's father, and I never asked.

It was possible that she was close to me in age, but the deep lines on her face, from years of hard work and pelting sun, made me believe otherwise. And, even though she only reached up to the top of my shoulder, I looked up to her. On days that we both had morning classes, Sarah and I rushed home to see Zubaida.

Zubaida often prepared a *tagine*—the name of both the clay dish and the meal served inside of it. One day, when we arrived home, she set the clay-bottomed dish on the table between us. Aromas of cinnamon, cumin, and ginger spun in the air as she pulled off the conical top, revealing a rabbit stew that had been colored with turmeric and cooked in a sauce of fresh onions, garlic, and tomatoes.

We tore small pieces from the crusty French baguette we had bought on the way home from school. We dipped the bread into the creamy, salty sauce. I talked about my day, savoring the complex flavors on my palate as I shared tidbits from my morning classes. When I was finished, Sarah would talk about her classes, peppering the same stories with different characters.

Sarah fished out an olive and then another. She popped them into her mouth. As I spoke, she sifted through the sauce with her bread. She twisted the round, clay tray in search of another olive. Her attempts were futile. She looked up at me—wide-eyed.

"Yep," I said. "There were only two."

She swallowed hard—gulping—as the second eye of the rabbit slid down her throat.

During my second year, one day as I walked to school, I was met with cold stares on the street. The year was 1985, the date was April 16. When I arrived at school, I went into the teachers' lounge.

"Did you hear the news?" one of the French teachers asked in English—a first. The French teachers at the school refused to speak any language other than their own, even though many of them spoke English much better then I spoke French.

"No," I said. "What happened?"

A number of other expatriate teachers had been standing in a huddle in the corner of the teachers' room. They came over to where I was standing with the French teacher. "Reagan bombed Libya," the French teacher said.

I stared back at him. I had neither a radio nor a television in my apartment. I had not heard the news. My site-mate did not have classes that morning. I was the only American at the school. As I passed through the courtyard on my way to my classroom, groups of students taunted me.

"*Les Américains, les assassins!*" Americans are assassins, the students in the courtyard shouted.

I continued walking. As I neared my classroom, I noticed that my students were milling about around the door. They were not lined up in single file as was custom each day before class. Taking a deep breath, I approached the doorway to the classroom.

I instructed the students to line up. They lazily fell into line. I stood outside the door, chin up, looking up and down the line. Previously, when I had invited them into the classroom, I had entered first, walking directly to my desk, depositing my materials before pulling out the lesson plan for the day.

As the students filed into the classroom, I stared at them. I slipped through the door and walked into the center of the room, where I stood staring sternly at any of the students who took too much time to settle into their seats. I crossed the room to my desk and pulled the class list out of my bag. As I took my place in front of the class, I felt the skin on my breastbone, back, and thighs harden. I stood for a moment, lips pursed. I called out each name—punctuating the air after each student had answered with a steely silence. When I was finished, I placed the class list on top of my desk and turned toward my students.

"Take out your copybooks," I said.

I looked at the students sitting in front of me. Their stares sliced through my steely façade, cutting into my broken heart. I had done everything that I could to learn about and respect their culture. But the US government had shown aggression

29

against their Muslim brothers and for this, as an American, in their eyes I was to carry the blame. For days afterward, my students looked at me as if it were I who had slipped out of my bed in the middle of the night, transporting myself east over the desert to drop the bombs that had fallen on Libyan soil.

I would live and work in many countries around the world from that day forward. Some cultures would appreciate Americans more than others. But no matter what I did, or who I was as an individual, I would always be associated with the actions of the US government, whether I supported what was being done politically or not.

Being overseas had taught me what it meant to be an American. I was proud of both my heritage and my country, but I was also frustrated. Although I knew that I would be seen as an extension of my own government overseas, I tried not to judge my national colleagues through the narrow lens of theirs.

In later years, I would provide humanitarian assistance in a number of countries where there had been a war. If I did not separate the people in these countries from the actions of their governments, it would be impossible for me to live and work productively alongside of them.

NOTES ON

The Boyfriend Sonnet

B rock was a water volunteer who lived in a coastal town in the south of Morocco. Following his initial training, he was issued a motorbike and sent to his site in Agadir, where he worked to install wells and water pumps. I learned that there was a new volunteer in the neighboring town where I had spent my initial two years in Morocco. But when I met Brock, I lived in the capital city.

I was instantly attracted to his rugged handsomeness. A country boy from Kentucky, he had studied engineering at Stanford University, and upon graduation, his father had given him a Rolex watch. Clanking it against the interior of wells, and scratching it on brass spigots, he wore it as if it were an old pair of sneakers. He said that it didn't matter, that it was only a watch. But the blood pulsing under the gold-plated timepiece, traveled directly from his wrist to his heart, keeping time in a country where time did not always matter.

Peace Corps volunteers, scattered in towns and villages across Morocco, traveled along dark mountain passes on overnight buses to meet up for parties on weekends. It was at one of these parties where I met Brock. Our first night together, as we sat on a rooftop in central Morocco, the moon cast wide shadows onto the cement walls around us as we talked late into the night.

During my third year, after extending to become a Peace Corps volunteer leader, I moved from Taroudant to the capital. I rented an apartment across from the train station in downtown Rabat. From my balcony, I could glimpse the wide boulevard that snaked along the king's palace. Inside the apartment, a wall of built-in shelves anchored a miniature cut-out of a painted kite in green and gold—an offering from my fellow volunteer and close friend Heather.

I spent the Christmas holidays that year in the south of Morocco with Heather and Brock. My gift from Brock was a ball of kite string procured from abroad. Back in Rabat, I attached the ball of string to the cut-out of the kite and looped it around the apartment. I attached the string to each corner of the room and placed the remaining ball—still ample—on the nightstand next to the mattress on the floor.

In February, I traveled to central Morocco to meet Brock. When he saw me his face lit up. Crossing the room, he placed a gift in my hand. He stood watching as I untied the bandana used to wrap the gift. I pulled out a solid, dense object fashioned with a blowtorch out of a brass water spigot. I looked up at him and smiled. In my hands, beads of brass sweat—dislodged from the blowtorch as it had melted the water spigot—textured a heavy heart.

Only one photo of the two of us remains. In the photo, we are sitting on the back of his motorbike outside of his apartment in Agadir. Behind us, the desert folds out onto a distant mountain chain. I am bracing myself on the back of the bike, twisting to look into the lens of the camera. Brock is sitting comfortably on the front of the bike, sporting a full beard and a well-worn leather jacket as he gazes over at me.

When Brock asked me to write him a sonnet, I crafted a poem void of iambic pentameter—an omission that he promptly pointed out upon first submission. I set out to be tutored by a fellow volunteer, learning the structure, cadence, and meter of a sonnet in both the Petrarchan (Italian) and Shakespearean (English) styles.

True to form, my first sonnet, "The Boyfriend Sonnet," consists of three quatrains and a rhyming couplet in iambic pentameter. The quatrains, however, employ a rhyming pattern of: *abba, cddc, effe*—a deviation from both the Italian and English styles.

Struggling to complete the third quatrain, I asked Brock for help. He offered the word "lucid" to refer to his demeanor, and the sonnet was complete.

Although I have had few regrets in my life, I regretted the manner in which I ended our relationship. When Brock suggested we become more serious, I left him. He had offered to meet me in France, where I was planning to go after I finished my Peace Corps service. Still in my twenties, I had wanted to fly solo.

A few years after I returned to the US, I tried to find Brock. I phoned a former volunteer, who had dated one of his friends, and asked her if she knew how I could get in touch with him. "Just a minute," she said, passing him the phone.

For years afterward, Brock thought that I had known where he was when I had placed the call. A fact that I denied, and he refused to believe, although it was, and remains, an innocent coincidence.

A number of years later, I wrote to Brock to apologize for the manner in which I had ended our relationship. I received a warmly written response, striking in its kindness. He had married and his job was going well. He had two boys. And he had forgiven me long ago.

I reread the message. When I was finished, I shut off my computer and closed the top. Brock had forgiven me, but I had yet to forgive myself.

THE BOYFRIEND SONNET

My boyfriend can't believe we live no lies
Unless, of course, he's hiding some inside.
For I, for one with time, can more than bide
And still accept the need to sever ties.
My vision thus comes weak while through my heart,
I gaze upon the things that set him high
Within my thoughts as I would like to try
To live today with love, though we must part.
What I may take from him I cannot tell,
Nor shall I tell the things that from the start
Became apparent not with eyes, but heart
Within a clear and icy lucid shell.
To one a lie, another missing truth,
To lie is young, to search a part of youth.

Rabat, Morocco, 1987

LONELY REFLECTION

Each day the morning brought a new surprise
For some. I waited but in vain to rip apart,
A thought, a gentle word, a lonely sigh,
Connecting you so far yet close in heart.
As months passed by I hardly knew I cared
As waxed light flickered, warming inner frost,
Then moments, gentle touching, two eyes paired
Brought back to mind a feeling never lost,
But freed. Though I feel empty I am full—
I want to dance alone and still be drawn
In circles—with your hand unroll the scroll
Of hushed words paled by distance, but not gone.
Return, and joy is mine though not for long,
For know I that with you I don't belong.

Rabat, Morocco, 1987

THE LATE NIGHT MOON

The moon followed me on a string last night,
And all the thoughts I had of you were lit.
Was it just moments that we sat, delight
Fullness, enticing, sleepy talk of wit?
Alone, we were together, then just two
Until I heard the sonnets from your flute
From deep within your soul, shrill sounds renew—
With tender notes of joy and love: your truth.
Is sorrow still as sweet if from the start,
Each moment mattered much more than was shown?
Two people predisposed before they part
To open hearts, to let each one be known.
I looked to you in hopes that you would be
That which I was not yet: in love with me.

Rabat, Morocco, 1987

SONNET CYCLE I

I.

I lay in bed then sat up with a start.
The Peace Corps was for me a time to seek;
To live and work abroad would set apart
A tourist from an optimistic freak.
A country that spoke French was what I sought
Though any place of need I said I'd do,
They said, "North Africa." I said, "Why not?"
Lest I regret that which I may accrue.
An early start the forms would need unless
I chose to get a job and keep my car
All of my trials and tribs I did confess
And if a skill I had no holds were barred.
For what I knew I got a TEFL[1] sight,
"I'll teach," I said and set off in the night.

II.

A small chalkboard and single piece of chalk
Did not prove to be all that I would use;
Upon arrival once I'd learn to mock
The methods aimed to teach those I'd amuse.
Charlie and I, we set up a small bar
With drinks to fill a need to make some cash,

---

1 Teaching English as a Foreign Language (TEFL)

37

After the hours of work Abla-Antar[2]
Served drinks to make a buck, but some got smashed.
By day we studied long and hard to speak
We practiced how to teach and how to stress
Importance upon those we'd meet each week,
We learned, they learned, we learned, they learned, I guess.
Off to the *bled*,[3] of Corps, of family,
"The toughest job," they said; I said, "We'll see."

III.
The bus rolled in, the sun rose, one more town
To pass before with luggage I would pant
To one I did not know, yet whom was known
Within the winding streets of Taroudant[4].
I found a *dar*[5] I liked with a sunroof.
I spent my nights alone, I wrote lessons,
The morning hours were filled with screams and proof
Of need of a few more feedback sessions.
When March arrived, I noticed all I knew
Did not relate to everything I did
Though I could see more clearly as I grew
From infant when in *stage*[6] to sixth-grade kid.
The first year gone, I hoped the next would be
A polished year of quiet, one with peace.

---

2 An epic love story of thirteenth-century Arab folklore. The bar that I managed with another volunteer in the common room of the training center was named Antar & Abla's. The bar was a cooperative to make money to buy alcohol at the swearing-in ceremony following our three-month training program, as this expense was not allowed with public monies per US Government regulations.

3 Countryside (Moroccan Arabic)

4 A small, walled city, one mile in circumference, built in the fourteenth century and located in the south of Morocco. Taroudant is often referred to as the *Son of Marrakesh*, a city in central Morocco known for its traders and covered labyrinth of small shops in the *medina*, large central market place.

5 House (Moroccan Arabic)

6 Technical training program (French)

IV.

The work, so hard at first, began to give
Goal one of Peace Corps reason did mature
I came to understand and learn to live,
Though of the culture I still wasn't sure.
I joined a club at school to learn the ropes
Of planning for a party—Throne Day[7] sort
They asked me of my talents, not my hopes.
My hand shot out toward young teacher of sport.
The crowd began to roar; it seemed absurd
He was my choice to lead us on our way,
At once it came—the meaning of the verb,
Not to direct, what instrument I played.
From then when I would speak or make demands,
I did a lot less talking with my hands.

V.

So far away is *stage,* is the first day
I landed on Moroccan sand that shone,
So close are those I met along the way
While passing through the culture I called home.
A third-year vet who travelled with advice
A box of books, a jug of wine or two,
Could never thank enough the vols so nice
To point me to *banquette*[8] as I passed through.
On going home: I'm only glad I stayed.
The things I now possess have taught me lots—
To care for more than simply getting paid,

---

7 Moroccan holiday on March 3 during the reign of King Hassan II to commemorate
independence in 1956 and King Hassan II's accession to the throne. Activities for
children were a focal point for celebration on this day. I worked with my students to write
and stage a play in English for the 1985 Throne Day festivities at the secondary school
in Taroudant, where I worked as an English teacher during my tenure as a Peace Corps
volunteer.

8 Back-less couch, with large pillows that sits on the floor. (French)

To take a risk or two, to call the shots.
Days full of goals and dreams under blue sky,
Night falls, stars melt to dawn as time goes by.

Rabat, Morocco, 1987

UNITED STATES OF AMERICA

Chapter Three

INTERNATIONAL INTERLUDE

Washington, DC 1988–95

W ithin weeks of returning to the US from Morocco, I was sent to the Eastern Shore of Virginia *to bring the world back home*, the third goal of the US Peace Corps. I had been selected to participate in a new program that the US Peace Corps was sponsoring stateside. For six weeks, I stayed with host families and gave presentations, recounting my Peace Corps experience to audiences ranging from kindergarten to the Rotary Club. Application for the program required a recommendation from my Peace Corps country director and submission of an essay.

Before departing for the Eastern Shore, I was invited to attend an orientation in Washington, DC. When I entered the meeting room, Kitty asked to speak to me. A former Peace Corps volunteer working for the national group of returned volunteers, she had been a member of the program selection committee.

"I loved your essay," she said.

Her long, dark hair, flowing skirts, and wedge sandals placed her in an era that I had missed by a few years growing up. I congratulated her on her new job. I had seen the posting for an education program coordinator based in Washington, DC. It was the type of job that I was seeking for myself.

The first week that I was in Virginia, Kitty wrote to tell me that she had grazed the shoulder of Jeff Bridges during a rally on the streets of Washington, DC. A venerable writer of great wit, Kitty's letters provided me with a refuge from the constant barrage of new faces each day. She understood what it was like to return home for the first time. In addition to her role as my mentor in the art of readjustment, we became fast friends.

When the program was completed, I returned to Minneapolis. I reached out to other newly returned volunteers from my group. Many of them had spent their initial months sitting alone for hours, feeling isolated after returning home. Once I was back in Minneapolis, I did the same.

I borrowed an electric typewriter, read through the English version of Victor Hugo's *Les Misérables,* noted all of the references to lightness and darkness, and typed them out. This activity filled three weeks.

I had been in Minneapolis without direction or work for three months when I called my friends Cathie and Peg. They offered to put me up for a few days in Washington, DC, while I followed up on job leads. A number of other friends from Morocco had relocated there as well. If I chose to relocate along with them, I would have a built-in support network.

My transition took longer than anticipated. Five weeks after arriving in Washington, DC, I moved into a house with two new roommates—an actress and a political activist. To expand my social network, I had sought out living arrangements with roommates that I had not previously known. My prospective roommates had liked my international background, immediately offering me the room as soon as the interview was over.

I held a series of temporary jobs with the US Peace Corps. Full-time employee positions with the US government required a more laborious hiring process. So, I slipped into temporary appointments, which could be filled more quickly. I worked as a training assistant and a training specialist in the Office of Training. I landed a temporary contract as the returned volunteer liaison in the Office of the Director, working alongside two others to support hundreds of newly returned volunteers seeking employment. The job that I held supporting other returned volunteers, however, would become my demise.

The director, a political appointee, had set his sights on elected office in his home state. As part of his duties, he regularly traveled throughout the US. I was asked to set up meetings with the former volunteers in states that he was visiting. Timelines were tight—he could only offer twenty minutes in the early mornings.

The leaders of the returned Peace Corps volunteer groups around the country were pleased to be invited to meet with the director no matter how short the duration. But many had young children, or other commitments that would not allow them to attend brief meetings scheduled at seven in the morning or earlier, often on short notice.

It was a Saturday morning when a group of returned volunteers held a meeting in the conference room at the Peace Corps office in Washington, DC. A senior staff member, who had been a volunteer, was slated to be in attendance. I had also been invited, as an observer. My supervisor was on leave. Out of courtesy, I asked a senior colleague, who oversaw my department, if she would like to attend the meeting with me.

After the morning session, my colleague called me aside. Visibly angry, she had wanted to address the group of former volunteers. As the participants filed out of the room for a scheduled lunch break, she ordered me to call them back. I spoke with the meeting facilitator. He began to corral the participants back into the room, but many had already left the building.

"It's too late now," I said to the facilitator. "We can arrange for her to speak as soon as everyone gets back from lunch."

My colleague left the meeting but did not return. The following Monday, I was called into her office. When I arrived, I was asked to wait in the reception area. After being ushered into her office by her assistant, my colleague waved me toward the guest chair in front of her wide desk. As her hand swept across her desk, it hit her coffee cup, spilling the hot, dark liquid on the papers piled in front of her. She called out to the woman manning the desk outside of her office to assist her in cleaning up the mess.

My colleague left the office with her coffee cup. As her assistant wiped down her desk, lifting papers one by one, patting them dry, I looked over my shoulder. My colleague had tacked up a number of pictures of herself with other political figures on the side wall of her office. In one of the photos, she was standing on the tarmac next to a private jet in a white fur coat. Her hand—extended—was grasping the hand of Richard Nixon. Other prominent Republicans also graced her walls.

My colleague returned to her office with a full cup of coffee. Bustling past me, she crossed the room and walked around the backside of her desk. Her assistant took the remaining pile of wet papers and left the room, closing the door behind her. The woman looked over at me—eyes bobbing as she took in my asymmetrical haircut.

"Why didn't you put me on the docket on Saturday?" she asked. She didn't wait for a response. "You left me sitting alone in the corner. I felt like a potted plant."

As she stared at me across her desk, I sat quietly.

"Well?" she said.

"I'm sorry," I said. "I didn't know that you had wanted to speak to the group." It was a mistake that I would regret for years afterward.

"And worse, there were only two people at the meeting with the director and the former volunteers in Charlotte last week," she said.

The meeting had been scheduled for Monday morning at 7:15 a.m. I had received the request to set up the meeting the previous Friday afternoon.

"The group wanted to meet the director," I said. "But many of the members in that area have young children and couldn't make the early meeting."

"It was your job to get them there," she said.

I sensed that she had been berated by the director for this.

"I thought there would be more than two people," I said.

"Are you calling me a liar?" she demanded.

I stared back at her. Her dark eyes reminded me of my mother's. I looked out the window. I thought of how willful my mother could be. I pulled on my mother's strength across the many states that lie between us. I looked back across the desk in front of me. I sat up.

"It was difficult to get people out to that location so early in the morning," I said.

"You are not committed enough for this job," she said. "You can go now."

I stood up to leave.

Two days later, I received a written notice from the human resource department. My temporary position had been terminated, effective immediately. I had been in the position for six months, and I had worked in other positions at headquarters for over two years. I had found a family in the Peace Corps— it was my home. Three days had remained on my temporary appointment when it was terminated—seventy-two hours. But I had made a mistake, and the cord had been cut swiftly.

As I looked for work I filled my days by volunteering at a small arts center that had recently opened in my neighborhood. While reading the *Washington Post* one morning, I stumbled on a review of *The Ponds of Kalambayi*, a book by Mike Tidwell, a Peace Corps volunteer who had written about his volunteer service in Zaire.

I called him.

"Hi Mike," I said. "This is Julie. I was a volunteer in Morocco. I read your review, and I'd like to organize a reading to promote your book."

We met to discuss the logistics. Prior to the event, I solicited donations from area restaurants. Many vendors were generous, resulting in a diverse sampling of international cuisine the night of the reading. I reached out to the returned Peace Corps volunteer community in the area, pulling more than fifty former volunteers into the art center on the night of the event.

The exhibit at the arts center on the evening of the reading included photographs and installations by local artists. The first week that I had worked at the art center, I had spent a considerable amount of time viewing the exhibit. From across the room, a photograph had caught my eye. Pink insulation sprouted around thick, wire rods hanging haplessly inside of the interior of a building. Trees in full bloom were framed by the open, partially demolished cement floors of the building. The title, typed onto a piece of paper attached to the photograph, read: PEACE CORP.

I had worked in the former Peace Corps office building some years earlier. Loret Miller Ruppe—one of the most engaged former Peace Corps directors—had hosted a small holiday party in her office. With a can of Miller beer in my hand, I stood outside on the balcony on the top floor of the building, looking out across Lafayette Park. From my perch, I could peer directly into the Oval Office of the White House. The direct angle, no doubt, the security reason the building had been demolished.

Standing in front of the photograph, I missed the Peace Corps like an old lover. I had wanted to purchase the print, but I could not afford it. Gazing at the debris resulting from the blast, the image mirrored my inner life. It would not be the first time, however, that I would come face-to-face with the spoils of a man-made disaster. In time, I would see similar images in many countries.

I was accepted into a master's degree program at the George Washington University. I added a subspecialty in business. Attending classes wrapped in a black-and-white Palestinian scarf and sporting a FREE THE FILES JFK button on the lapel of my coat, my fellow students in international education were representatives from ministries of education from around the world, former Peace Corps volunteers, and the wives of Arab diplomats. The students in my business classes were both military personnel and civilians seeking MBAs.

I took a class in group dynamics. The instructor, a man in his early forties, had been a trainer in transcendental meditation in the seventies. The first night of class, he spoke of his work with couples when he was a trainer, recounting the power he had experienced by making men cry. I looked around the classroom, no one else seemed shocked.

"Excuse me," I said, raising my hand. "I just want to say that there are other approaches to training." I continued, "I was a trainer for the Peace Corps, where we used a model of 'challenge and support' when working with new volunteers." The instructor stared back at me.

The following week, the instructor asked, "What is the bottom line?" Everyone had agreed, "Making money."

The instructor wrote the response on the board.

"Excuse me," I said, looking around the room. "I work for a nonprofit organization. The *mission* is the bottom line, although we need to conduct our activities professionally, since we have a responsibility to our donors."

Without comment, the instructor continued, posing a new question on the basics of business.

During the third week of the course, the class was instructed to meet weekly in designated groups, observe the interrelationships of group members, and note the outcomes. "If you are prone to be a leader, sit back and let others take control," he told the class. "Your final project can be a PowerPoint presentation, a group discussion, or a poem," he said. "Be creative."

He dismissed the class.

The first night that our group met, the sergeant and I exchanged words. He looked at my FREE THE FILES JFK button. There was a movement to open classified files from the Kennedy administration prior to the usual fifty-year waiting period.

"Do you think our government would lie to us?" he asked.

"Uh, Agent Orange," I replied.

"People like you make the hair stand up on the back of my neck," he said.

The sergeant was my age. While I had served in the Peace Corps, extending for an additional year as a volunteer leader following my initial two-year commitment, he had served in the army. During our first meeting, the sergeant and I each vied to chair it.

"Let's try not to dominate the group, like the instructor suggested," the sergeant said.

I looked back at him.

"Okay," I said. "I'll try."

The meeting swirled aimlessly, but the sergeant and I remained true to our agreement. The group decided to go camping. At the end of the meeting, the sergeant and I looked at each other. I shrugged my shoulders, he rolled back his eyes.

The night of the camping trip, we met outside of the sergeant's home, bundled our gear together, and piled into two cars. I was in the truck being driven by the sergeant. He put his truck into reverse, backed it out of the driveway, and stopped.

"I forgot my gun," he said, pulling the truck back into the driveway.

A feeling of uneasiness washed over me.

"I'm sorry, but I'm not comfortable going camping with a gun," I said.

"We don't know what we'll be faced with out there."

"But, we're going to a national park," I said.

He opened the door of the truck and went into his house. When he returned, his weapon was concealed.

The night of our final presentation, while other groups used PowerPoint presentations, our group performed a skit with props and a poem that I had written. As suggested, I had urged the group to be creative. Yet, following our presentation, our group was applauded with blank stares from both our classmates and the instructor.

In graduate school, I learned that I did not fit in. I missed the many associations that I previously had had with other like-minded friends and colleagues outside of the US. Remaining in the US, where I would be expected to follow strict cultural norms in order to succeed in life was not an option for me. I yearned for the freedom of living and working in a more culturally rich environment that, until that point, I only had found overseas.

When I was ready to leave my Washington, DC desk job, I sent out ten résumés to the most influential people that I knew. I had worked for a member agency of a consortium of international organizations, serving as co-chair on one of the committees. Through this work, I had met senior managers in several organizations. When I was ready to find a position overseas, these were the people that I reached out to for assistance.

I applied for a position in Rwanda. The recruiter told me that the salary and other terms were non-negotiable. This struck me as odd. The ability to negotiate is one of the most important skills for a director in insecure, post-conflict environments. Nevertheless, I accepted the position and was deployed to Kigali.

I felt fortunate to land the job. During my job search, my criteria had been to become the representative of an international organization in a country where French was spoken. I had succeeded. But I also knew that the real reason that I had been offered the job was that no one else had wanted to go there.

RECKLESS ABANDON

Amber leaves burnt slightly by the sun,
Rumpled and tossed aside await the breath
Of dawn. Light winds scatter them one by one
As children stomp the leaves to dust.
The gray powder is soon forgotten by
Eyes that once understood the complex hue
Of night. Dark skin shining, the empty sky
Greets night's painful demise with a new moon.
If we are to live with reckless abandon
As children who play aimlessly must do—
Be wise must we to not only have fun,
But careful to learn well the rules of truth.
A withered branch bursts forth with buds that please,
The wake of spring and fall of amber leaves.

Washington, DC, 1992

SANS MES RÊVES

J'ai commande une bière.
Il fait nuit.
Je l'ai regardé
Jusqu'à ce que la musique
Commencer jouer.

Il y a longtemps
Que j'attendais
Qu'il m'emmène
Vers le ciel plein
D'étoiles.

Nous sommes partis
A la sauvette.
Mais quand
Je me suis réveillée,
Je me suis trouvée,

Seule, sans mes rêves.

Washington, DC, 1992

WITHOUT MY DREAMS

(Translation from French to English)

I ordered a beer.
It was dark.
I watched it
Until the music
Began to play.

A long time
I waited
For him to take me
Toward the star filled skies

We left
Swiftly and furtively.
But when I awoke
I found myself

Alone, without my dreams.

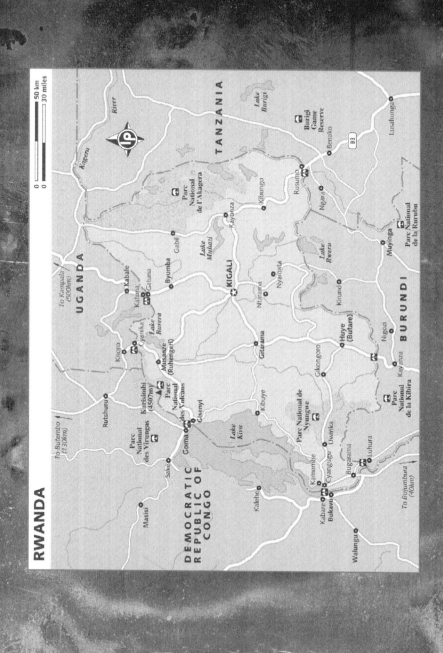

RWANDA

Chapter Four

AFTER THE GENOCIDE

Kigali 1995–97

Before I departed for Rwanda, I watched a news story of the genocide on television. In the background of the shot, as the commentator reported the story, the head of a man rolled off of his shoulders and onto the ground. It was as if a bowling ball had been dropped off of the top of his body.

When I arrived in Kigali, eighteen months after the genocide, there was still dried blood on the curtains in my bedroom. But I had clean sheets and towels—my colleagues before me had slept on dirty, bloodied mattresses. Before I left the US, many of my friends and colleagues had warned me of the complexities of the political situation. Many wondered if I had the ability to manage in such a difficult environment.

In Kigali, I immediately understood what they had meant. As soon as I landed, everyday life took on a deeply disturbing hue that remained with me throughout my stay. In the backyard of our guesthouse there was a vegetable garden. Before the rains, bodies had been stacked six feet high, settling into the earth as they decomposed into the soil. One evening before dinner, while he was weeding in the garden, my colleague unearthed a femur. The essence of death permeated the soil around us, composting memories impossible to escape.

After traveling for two days, I arrived late in the night. I was met by a colleague, who brought me to the guesthouse. As we drove through the dark streets, my colleague informed me that Mary Robinson, the president of Ireland, was speaking to the international community at the Ministry of Labor and Social Affairs (MINITRASO) the following morning. As I grabbed my bags from the back of the truck, I arranged to be picked up in time to attend the meeting the next day. I had read about Mary Robinson, and I admired her commitment to humanitarian issues.

The next morning when I arrived at the ministry, there was already a long line of white Toyota Land Cruisers parked along the dirt road. Many of them were backed into their spaces, ready to jet out at a moment's notice. I later learned that this was customary protocol for security reasons. And, over the years, I learned to drive a Land Cruiser as easily backward as forward.

The outside of the building was sparse and dirty-gray. Although it was sunny and bright outside, little of the natural sunlight filtered into the building. There was no electricity. The empty light fixtures, even if they had had bulbs, would not have been able to provide illumination. The meeting room had one long table and a spattering of old wooden chairs, many in disrepair. Three of the nicest chairs were placed behind the table in official fashion. Representatives from the international community huddled around the table and against the walls, chatting idly as they waited for the president of Ireland to arrive.

Mary Robinson entered the dark room. The Rwandan Minister of Social Affairs and his humanitarian coordinator entered behind her. The Irish Minister of Development, also a woman, accompanied the president. I had expected to hear prepared comments, but instead Mary Robinson told the assembled crowd that she had come to listen and learn. She briefly outlined her commitment to the reconstruction of Rwanda, reaffirming her stand on human rights—including the rights of women—before opening up the discussion to questions.

I was introduced to a number of representatives of international organizations. Eva, who worked for a Danish organization, went out of her way to welcome me, offering any assistance that I might need as I got settled. Later that afternoon, I learned that her organization rented one of the larger rooms in our office complex. From that first day, we worked closely together on a daily basis. We became fast friends. For the duration of my time in Rwanda, she was also my confidant.

After the meeting, I went to the office where many pressing needs awaited my immediate attention. Initially, I worked with the team to address deep-seated management issues that had been set aside in the early months of the emergency response. The initial skeleton staff had responded to the larger humanitarian needs—they had saved lives. I organized the administration and finance departments. I drafted policies and procedures and instituted them throughout program sites. I monitored the larger political and advocacy issues affecting the work of the international agencies on the ground.

Humanitarian aid groups worked closely with the agencies that were clearing landmines. During the protracted conflict, landmines had been laid willy-nilly throughout the country. Concentrations of both anti-personnel, and the larger, anti-tank landmines, were planted along the borders where the Rwandan Patriotic Front had been advancing prior to signing the Arusha Accord in 1992.

Although the main roads had been demined, landmines were often washed up with the rains. Located near the equator, it rained daily in Rwanda. As the director, I was expected to sit in the front right side of the vehicle, a place of both honor and chance. If a driver unknowingly rolled over one of the small disks, the front right side of the vehicle would be the first part of the vehicle to be destroyed.

The level of stress was suffocating. As the weeks wore on, I began to doubt my abilities. When faced with a difficult decision, I would ask myself what my former boss would have done. She had been a financial controller and a program director. She understood what was needed in the field to ensure professional programming. I drew from her experience when stumped, remembering how she had handled issues when I had worked with her in Washington, DC.

I struggled to understand the political environment. To cope, I looked within the larger international community and identified colleagues with strong analytical skills. Patty was twenty-five years old when I met her. Wise beyond her years, her ability to provide no-nonsense analysis in understandable language was invaluable to countless organizations. I relied on her to help me understand the political context, and as a result, I was able to make better management decisions. Patty rose quickly through the ranks, and in later years, I would happily work directly for her. But in Rwanda, she was my advisor and my friend.

I had professional support from colleagues on the ground, but I needed an inner sense of purpose to shield against the daily barrage of tragedy and sorrow. On a Sunday morning, when I found myself alone in the staff house, I poured a cup of coffee and walked out into the yard.

Months earlier, the yard had been riddled with stacks of bones. Before we had rented the house, it had been the annex for an emergency hospital. Hundreds of people had died and been buried there. After the first rainy season, the bones had settled into the ground, and a light covering of earth had begun to grow over them. I walked around the garden, making peace with the wide, shallow grave that had become my home.

I had been ill prepared to take on such an important position. I asked myself why I had come to Rwanda. If I was going to stay, I needed to determine what my contribution was going to be. As I stood sipping my coffee, I decided that there were only two things that I could do—be fair and consistent. By doing so, I believed that I could stabilize the outer working environment for my staff as they grappled with their inner trauma.

I had arrived with strong planning and coordination skills. In time, I also accumulated an arsenal of my own management skills to draw upon when I needed to make decisions. But during my early months in Rwanda, it was the wisdom and integrity of Bonnie Ricci that I initially relied upon to pull me through.

The security situation was tenuous. There were reports that vehicles were being stopped outside of Kigali, and Tutsis were summarily being shot. Many of my staff members were ethnic Tutsi, and I was concerned that I would not be able to keep them safe while they were on the road.

I called a senior director at the home office to discuss my fears. She told me not to worry. The national staff, she had said, understood well the risks involved in working with an international organization. Her advice did little to calm my fears. My national staff would always be at risk.

I met with my national staff regularly to discuss the security situation. I asked for their insights so that I could better understand the context from their perspective. As a result, key national staff became trusted, cultural advisors.

Assumpta, my assistant, had been an officer in the Rwandan Patriotic Front. She kept my schedule and aided me in all aspects of my work, including writing letters for me in French. She was extremely disciplined, holding herself and her colleagues to a high degree of professionalism. She fought for rights and benefits for the national staff with a determination and verve that I respected and admired. She thought things before I did, reminding me where I needed to be and what I needed to do. And, she made me laugh.

I worked with the team to revise the salary scale. Assumpta approached me for a promotion and a raise. I denied her request. She came to me a second time to discuss the issue. Again, I denied her. The third time she approached me, she made such a persuasive and acceptable argument, I agreed.

The work was never-ending. I built a professional network with other international organizations and key government officials. I partnered with a number of government agencies to address shared issues. Together, we organized an international seminar on children's rights. I learned how intricately aligned the Rwandans were. Accessing keynote speakers and confirming commitments from high-level government officials was easily facilitated. Invited guests and speakers were brothers or cousins of the team of organizers.

Expatriates explored Rwanda, arranging visits to see the mountain gorillas, rafting down the Ruganwa River, or spending time at a nearby lake on weekends. I tended to stay close to home. I arrived in Kigali in September and remained in country over the Christmas holidays to assure staff that I was serious about my work with them on the ground.

We held an office Christmas party. The menu was continental, including roasted beef and potato salad. The second year was different. The planning committee was provided with enough money to buy three goats, which they roasted and served with cold beer and fried bananas. The previous year, before I had known better, the staff had chosen a menu to appease the handful of expatriates. As I spent more time in the culture and learned what was traditionally preferred, I made adjustments. To this day, like many Rwandans—and many other East Africans—I love roasted goat and fried bananas.

I was invited to take a short rafting trip in an inflatable dinghy. Two of my colleagues had taken a weekend trip with the captain of the dinghy a month earlier. They had floated back to Kigali from a point well outside of the city, marveling as they later recalled the beauty along the riverbanks. They spent two days on the river, camping for a night in a village along the banks. My experience would be different.

It was Sunday morning when I met up with the crew. I arranged to be dropped off at the home of one of the passengers at seven in the morning. Two of my friends from the UN had also been invited to join the group. With the captain and two others, there were six passengers.

We drove for two hours to reach the launch site. Upon arrival, we loaded the dinghy. Collectively, we had six bottles of orange Fanta and a block of white cheese. By ten o'clock, we were floating peacefully on the narrow river. At noon, we cracked open the orange sodas and passed around small wedges of cheese, laughing and joking as we hit rapids so subtle we could hardly feel the blip as we passed over them.

The dinghy was the circumference of a large kitchen table. We sat on the inflated outer lip of the craft. The captain sat inside, nestled against the rear, casually manning the small motor. Every so often, the motor would stop sputtering, presumably shut off to save fuel as we continued to float quietly toward Kigali.

At two o'clock, I wondered how much longer we would be afloat. I had not prepared to be out for the entire day. When I asked the captain how far he thought it would be to our final destination, he shrugged. A usually jovial and talkative character, I was surprised by his aloofness. I asked him if we had passed the place where he and my colleagues had camped along the river. He evaded my question.

I continued to prod him. He admitted that we had not reached the campsite that they had used on their previous trip. I asked how he had determined where we would put in for the shorter trip. He hemmed and hawed, before conceding that he had used the same launch site he had chosen for the longer, weekend trip. I stared back at him. It was late afternoon. None of the crew had adequate clothing to guard against the approaching night chill.

The sky took on a mauve hue. Strips of clouds painted in long strokes connected the tips of two mountains in the distance. Each time we rounded a turn in the river, I asked if we had passed the campsite signaling the halfway point of the previous trip. The captain had not traveled with my colleagues after dark. There were wild animals along the river, and the bridges were manned with armed soldiers.

The sun began to set as we neared a bridge in a remote outpost. Two soldiers with machine guns signaled us ashore. My friend from the UN told us to remain in the dinghy. He had a plan. He disembarked and mounted the steep hill along the riverbank. As he spoke to the soldiers, he pointed to the dinghy. With his hands, he explained that we had lost our way. His plan, however, had proven to be a daunting task—he spoke little French and no Kinyarwanda, the local language.

The soldiers signaled the entire group of passengers to disembark and climb the riverbank. My friend kept waving his arms wildly, repeating, "UN, UN!" The soldiers asked him if we had guns. He said that we were unarmed. In unison from the dinghy below, we all raised our hands. One of the crew pointed to the inside of the empty cooler. In exasperation, the soldiers relented. Our emissary slid down the hill and into the dinghy, and we quickly shoved off from the shore.

Night fell without the rising of the moon. We floated soundlessly as the river continued to open up in front of us in an unending channel of darkness. The air continued to cool. We rounded another bend. Tall pine trees reached into the sky, searching for the stars. But they had fallen to earth. Thousands of fireflies illuminated the trees on the shores beside us.

Rounding another bend, two mountain peaks poked out of the clouds in the distance. An airplane, miniature in scope, descended between them. Kigali! My initial excitement quickly turned to despair as I calculated the distance that still lay ahead.

As we neared a particularly shallow area on the river, I heard a loud "Pharumph!" Earlier in the evening we had nicknamed ourselves with the characters from *Gilligan's Island*, a popular television program in the US in the seventies. Ginger tightened her grip on the outside of the dinghy, as did I, Mary Ann. The Professor and Mr. Howell slipped off the outside perimeter into the center of the dinghy and braced themselves against the empty cooler.

The captain remained calm, relaxing in his inner sanctum against the rear end of the dinghy. We heard loud snorting and splashing, but it was too dark to make out the shapes until we were directly beside the large, wide bodies. Days later, I would learn that hippos eat more people in Africa than any other animal, including crocodiles. A fact I was happily unaware of as we passed the bloat, out for their nightly feeding.

It had been dark for hours, and we were still miles from Kigali. My hopes of safely returning home dimmed as the sparkling light of the fireflies also dimmed beside me. Even so, the tension in the dinghy began to dissipate. We had skirted the hippos.

Leaving the crevasse of the two mountains in our wake, we twisted through another bend. At once, we all saw it—a bridge. It was sure to be manned with military, but we had no means to signal that we were not foe. We decided on a course of action. So as not to be mistaken as rebels who had crossed the nearby border, Ginger and I spoke loudly in English as we passed under the bridge. Rambling on about mundane topics, we continued our rant until, without incident, we passed safely under the bridge.

Once again, the dinghy fell quiet as we continued to follow the channel. Breaking the silence, I shared a hopeful thought. "We don't have to worry," I said. "My colleague will be there."

I turned to face the captain.

"He will meet us at the point in the river where you ended your weekend trip," I said. "I'm sure of it."

I explained to the crew that because I was so late returning to the staff house, my colleague would call the driver to ask where we had launched the dinghy. I said that he would calculate the time that he had spent on the two-day trip during daylight hours to determine when he would need to be at the other end to meet us.

"He will call out to us from the riverbank, so we will know where to dock the dinghy in the darkness," I told the crew. "He will be there to pull us up the muddy shore." I was silent for a moment before adding, "He will be there."

And he was.

The next day when work resumed, professional challenges continued to come my way. Conflict management was an ongoing need. Rumors circulated among national staff throughout the organization. Emotions ran high as my staff recalled who had done what to whom, perceived or otherwise. Anger, which was not normally openly displayed in the culture, boiled over into rare shouting matches as my colleagues continued to grapple with their trauma.

I was alerted that there was a problem in the program office. One of the female staff members was threatening to harm another. When I entered the room, a young female staff member was hurdling accusations—arms flailing—in preparation for an assault on her colleague. I told the young woman to stop and ordered her to my office. She reluctantly backed off.

As she entered my office, I told her to sit down. I asked her to tell me about what had happened. She told me that I was not African and that I could never understand. I told her that she was right, I was not African. But one thing was clear—if she wanted to start a fight, she needed to take it outside of the office compound. She argued with me, reiterating my lack of understanding. I reminded her that she had signed a code of conduct, which did not permit aggression among staff members. I told her that if she persisted, she would be fired.

It would take many more interventions among staff before I was able to dispel aggressive behavior at the office. One incident in particular was a turning point. A staff member was terrorizing many of the other staff. As a former member of the Rwandan Patriot Front, he had strong ties to the military government. He demanded drivers and other staff to provide him with personal services. He used organizational resources for his personal pleasure and gain. By the time the situation came to my attention, it was out of control.

Suleiman, the head of logistics, had learned of the issue and began to deny his requests. This incensed the staff member. Suleiman was not known to have any direct ties to the genocide. Our colleague was not deterred, facilitating the jailing of Suleiman without cause. After a month in jail, he was summarily released, but not before suffering beatings so severe he was left with a concussion.

Upon his release, Suleiman requested to be transferred out of the country. I discussed the issue with my regional director, but we were not able to provide him with a safe haven. I called Suleiman into my office. I told him that I understood his situation, but the organization could not provide him with work outside of Rwanda.

I continued to follow the performance of the colleague who had arranged to have Suleiman jailed. For months, his performance had been lacking. He did not complete his tasks. He spread rumors about the organization when he was in the field on official site visits. I documented his poor performance and provided him with warning letters that were also placed in his file.

The situation continued to deteriorate. I prepared the final warning letter on a Friday afternoon. Per local labor law, with the third warning letter, I could also legally terminate a staff member for non-performance. I considered my options carefully. If I terminated this person, it was possible that he would retaliate against Suleiman or the other staff members. Yet, if I didn't respond appropriately, he would continue to terrorize the staff.

On Monday morning, I arrived at the office with resolve. I called the rogue staff member to my office and asked him to sit down. I presented him with his third warning letter and informed him that he was terminated for non-performance. He signed the third letter and angrily left my office. I immediately called Suleiman into my office. I told him what I had done and that I could not ensure his safety.

I was worried. I have met thousands of people in my life time, managing over one hundred international and thousands of national staff throughout my career. During this time, I have only met and worked with a very distinct handful of people whom I would term abusive, deranged, or cruel. I grieved the potential loss of Suleiman from the team. He had always been a steadfast and dependable colleague. I trusted and respected him. More importantly, I needed him.

Throughout the day, I feared for his safety. Emotions were still so raw among so many Rwandans that one could not anticipate the potential irrationality of others, especially those with direct connections to the military. I told Suleiman that I understood if he felt that for his own personal safety he would need to flee the capital or the country.

That evening when I returned home, I was struck by my own vulnerability. I had not fully considered the effects that my decision could have on my own security. I religiously drove with locked doors, walking around the vehicle to ensure that it was secure before entering it. I backed into parking spots. I had a guard at my house both day and night, but the guard was not armed. Anyone wielding an AK-47 could force entry into my home.

The next day, Suleiman returned to work. He came into my office, as he did every morning, to brief me on the overall security situation and outline the logistical needs of the day. I smiled warmly and thanked him for returning. I asked him if he was sure that he wanted to stay. He nodded before resuming the discussion of the pressing tasks at hand.

As I took my daily stroll through the office that day, chatting briefly with staff from each department, I noticed a considerable decrease in the tension that had previously permeated the office. I also sensed something deeper—an unspoken acknowledgement of relief. Their colleague, who had instilled fear in them, was gone.

To be accused of genocide crimes, one did not merely need to be seen killing another person. One could also be accused of complicity. If three people made statements against an accused person, an arrest could be made. During the genocide, the central government had encouraged the massacres through state-run radio broadcasts. A Rwandan journalist later admitted to inciting the violence. In one of her broadcasts on *Radio Mille Collines*—radio of a thousand hills—she had implored listeners to cut what she termed cockroaches into pieces with a machete.

The Belgians had coddled the Tutsis, providing educational opportunities and political advancement to the monarchy to cement their colonial power. The favoritism had incensed the Hutus, thwarting numerous attempts at power sharing between the Tutsis and the Hutus as the country prepared for independence, which was granted in 1962.

With independence came power for the Hutus. With power came abuses. This led ethnic Tutsis to seek refuge over the border. For generations, displaced Tutsi populations lived in refugee camps where the Tutsi-dominated Rwandan Patriotic Front (RPF) was spawned. Prior to the onset of the genocide on April 7, 1994, negotiations to broker a peace between the RPF and the Hutu government of Rwanda had been progressing.

The Tutsi-dominated Rwandan Patriotic Front had been camped out in a ring around Kigali, outside of a ring of government police, a ring of military, and a ring of UN Peacekeepers, respectively, per a negotiated peace agreement prior to the commencement of the genocide. The Hutu hardliners vehemently objected to the additional concessions that were being negotiated by the president. As the military of Habyarimana's government had been camped at the airport, readily able to launch the missiles that had downed the plane carrying the president as it prepared to land, speculation arose that the event was a coup by Hutu extremists who resented the president's overtures toward power sharing with the Tutsis.

The hate campaigns that had been initiated months earlier by the Hutu government increased. *Radio Milles Collines*, the radio station that aired propaganda to fuel the massacres, had been launched in 1993 by relatives of Hutu President Juvénal Habyarimana. Following the downing of a plane carrying the president in April 1994, government-trained militia, the *Interahamwe*—those who attack together—launched the state-sanctioned massacres of minority ethnic Tutsis and politically moderate Hutus.

For months, a killing spree ensued, as husbands killed wives, priests killed parishioners, and children killed neighbors alongside the militias. The RFP moved in, capturing the capital city of Kigali to end the mass killing, but not before the estimated death toll had reached just under one million slain.

Over two million refugees flowed over the borders into neighboring countries, many in fear of retribution. Former Hutu government officials and military personnel used the moving populations as a human shield, crossing the border and settling into the refugee camps, where they continued to wield power.

In Rwanda, the staff and I worked with children, fostering them in communities where they had lost parents to the genocide. We provided small income-generation activities for families and community members supporting unaccompanied and orphaned children. Children under three years of age were allowed to be placed with their mothers in prison to enable the mother to create a bond with her child. To accommodate these children, a special space was allotted in each of the women's wards. We worked in all twelve provinces to provide supplemental nutrition to children living with their incarcerated mothers, providing the mothers with seeds for small gardens and cows for milk.

The women accused of genocide were imprisoned in their home provinces, allowing family members to visit them and bring additional food. As few families had sufficient resources to adequately provide for their children at home, any offerings that they could provide to their family members in prison were meager. At the age of three, children staying in the prison with their mothers were united with family members or fostered in their home communities. To ensure that the children continued to have their minimum nutritional needs met, we provided assistance to them once they had been united with their families in their communities.

The justice system was overwhelmed—few of the women who had been in prison since their arrest had had access to legal representation. The hundreds of thousands of people accused of genocide could potentially spend years languishing in prison, with little or no chance of ever being tried.

When we arrived at the prison, the women were striking. Tin cups banged against the metal bars of the windows opening onto the central courtyard. We had come to visit the women in the family section of the women's ward. The men's ward, where prisoners were crowded into areas where they had standing room only, was across the courtyard.

The women were able to lie down to sleep. Large, wooden bunk beds were stacked three high along the side walls of the main room, blocking out any natural light from the small, barred windows. Four latrines were located in a small, shaded outdoor enclosure off of the large central room where most of the three hundred women were held. Meals were prepared by the women themselves in large metal pots, simmering on small fires in the outdoor enclosure.

I prepared to enter the women's ward with the program coordinator. As the director of the prison unlocked the wooden door to the ward, the clanging of tin cups rose to a crescendo in anticipation of our entry. When the door was opened, a river of women parted as we entered the large room. As we walked along the center of the room, the swell of women formed a single mass around us. I heard the door close and lock behind me.

My colleague, a frequent visitor to the prison, walked with confidence and ease. I held my head steady while keeping my countenance serene as I walked pass hundreds of women accused of genocide, many with little or no hope of ever being freed from prison in their lifetimes.

We continued through the large room to a smaller room at the back of the unit, where fifty mothers were being held with their children. It was not as dark as the central area had been—the beds were not blocking the sunlight that flowed through the windows. A second outdoor enclosure was located off to the side of the family section. The mothers maintained a small garden in this area to supplement the diets of their children. We were offered a corner of a wooden bed. As I turned to sit, a small child saw my face and shrieked. Pulling back my head, surprised, I expected that it was the first time that he had ever seen blue eyes.

The meeting began with an update on the supplemental nutrition activities for the children of the detainees. Once the program coordinator had completed her official business, the women began to talk. Many were agitated as they outlined their demands, which they asked us to communicate to the prison director. They wanted to have direct communication with their husbands in the men's ward. They appreciated the support for their children, but they wanted larger portions of rice and other staples that they combined for their communal meals. They needed firewood for cooking and cleaning supplies for the latrines. They wanted longer and more frequent visiting hours than the short weekly visits currently allowed.

The women knew that we could not change their situation. But aside from the weekly visits from a representative of the International Committee of the Red Cross, they had no one to talk to about their grievances. We continued to listen quietly, noting their issues and demands. When the women were finished, we agreed to pass the information on to the prison officials.

We got up to leave. The sea of women in the central room parted to allow us to pass through. And, as the sea had closed behind us when we had entered, it closed behind us as we moved through the room to depart. I maintained my neutral expression, trying not to convey the slightest expression lest it be interpreted as fear.

Outside, the day was sunny and bright. I climbed into the white Land Cruiser. The two-hour drive back to the office had a calming effect as we traveled quietly through the hilly mountainside, green and plush as far as the eye could see. The fear I had experienced began to dissipate, as if floating freely out of the back of the vehicle through the exhaust.

I thought of the demands of the mothers. If the time I had spent listening to them had allowed them to vent their frustrations on someone other than their children—if only for a few hours—the stress that I had endured during the visit had been worthwhile.

The vehicle neared the gate of the office compound. I turned toward the backseat to thank the program coordinator for arranging the visit. I asked her what her work plan was for the coming week. The program coordinator outlined the supplies she needed to procure and distribute to four other prisons by the end of the week. She told me that many of the children were nearing the age of three, and arrangements were underway to unite them with their extended families within the surround ing communities.

I turned and waved to the guard as he opened the gate. I took a deep breath and sank back into my seat. The driver gunned the engine in preparation to mount the steep drive. It was early evening, but my day was not yet finished.

As I climbed the stairway leading up to the office, my eye caught the mauve hue of the sunset. I stopped for a moment to take it in. As I stood watching, the sun slid out of sight behind the hillside in the distance. Once inside, I continued my climb up the internal stairway, propelling myself with each breath as my mind turned to the dozens of new e-mail messages that would be waiting.

Malaria, although present throughout the country, was not rampant due to the altitude. Another disease had taken hold of the population. It was the early years of HIV/AIDS. The organization I worked with provided basic health services in rural areas outside of Kigali. But when staff started losing weight at drastically short intervals in the capital city, it became apparent that they, too, needed services.

In conflict environments, rape is used as a tool of war. Coupled with promiscuity, the disease had spread widely in Rwanda. At the time, the government of Rwanda had little experience or capacity to diagnose and provide treatment for the disease. Without detection, those who had contracted the HIV virus often experienced a sudden decline into full-blown AIDS.

I was scheduled to return to the US over the Christmas holidays when Assumpta invited me to her home for coffee. I was delighted to spend some time with her outside of the office. Even more, I was honored to have been invited to her home. It was only the second invitation that I had received from one of my national staff since arriving in Rwanda.

I had been in Rwanda for over a year. When I was still new to the culture, I was looking at a map of Rwanda with Assumpta. Visitors were arriving from the home office, and Assumpta was preparing a welcome packet of information for them. She asked me to review the contents. I pulled out the map from the packet, opened it up, and laid it out on the table in front of me. Assumpta pointed to Ruwengeri and told me that her family had lived in the northwesterly province before fleeing to Uganda in 1959. I asked her where her family had gone after they left the refugee camp.

"They are all dead," she said, laughing nervously.

When I arrived at Assumpta's house, the door was open. She was standing at the end of a long hallway. When she saw me, she motioned me to enter. Although she was dressed casually, she still sported her signature scarf, which she always wore around her neck. We sat in the garden and drank instant coffee, chatting briefly about work and my imminent departure to the US. When she stood, I noticed that the belt cinched around her waist was drawn in tightly, and the size of her waist, which previously had been proportionate to my own medium frame, was much smaller. We had already lost two staff members to HIV/AIDS, both suffering a swift and rapid decline.

After a short visit, I got up to leave, and Assumpta walked me to my car. I opened the door to the car and reached inside. Pulling out a small package, I handed it to Assumpta. I told her that I was sorry that she had lost all of her family, including her sisters, in the genocide. I said that my sister, Kristine, had given me a beautiful green-print scarf before I had departed from the US to Rwanda. I asked her if she would accept the scarf as a gift from my sister. I said that I was sure that my sister would be honored if she would accept it. Assumpta smiled shyly as I placed the scarf in her hands. Without speaking, she turned and walked toward the entryway of her house. After she had passed through the door, I climbed into the car, started the engine, and drove away.

The noticeably diminished size of Assumpta's waist haunted me while I was on leave. I feared the worst. When I returned to Rwanda after the holidays, Assumpta was not in the office. Nor was she in Kigali. She had fallen ill while I was away, leaving Kigali to seek treatment in a hospital in Uganda near the refugee camp where she had grown up. I asked Josepha, our receptionist, if we could call her. I wanted to ask Assumpta if she needed anything or if we could arrange to support her in any way.

Josepha dialed the number, using the international line located at the front reception area. When the call connected, she passed me the phone. I had to speak loudly, almost yelling, to counteract the poor quality of the connection. I asked her how she was, and although she responded that she was fine, her voice was so weak I could hardly make it out. I told her that we were all thinking of her, and I asked her if there was anything that we could do for her. She thanked me and said that she needed to go.

I looked toward the pool of assistants seated nearby in the open front office area, pleading with my eyes for them to tell me what else I should say.

"I love you!" I yelled loudly before dropping the phone into Josepha's outstretched hand.

Josepha sat gripping the earpiece, looking up at me before slowly placing it back on its cradle. The staff continued to look on quietly. Such an open display of emotion was rare in a culture where the most intimate form of greeting was the grasping of each other's elbows—a show of physical contact reserved for the closest of family members or dearest of friends. I had only observed this greeting on a few occasions while out in the field with colleagues.

Verbal exclamations of affection were virtually unknown in the culture. Public displays of grief were unheard of, even after the most traumatic experiences. But Assumpta was dying, and I knew that I would never see her again.

As Assumpta lay dying, the buzz picked up over the return of more than a million refugees from across the border in Zaire. Preparations were underway for large movements of returning refugees in the coming days or weeks—no one could predict precisely when the influx would begin.

The former government officials and *Interhamwe* had held the refugees hostage as a protective shield in the camps. Few refugees had been able to leave the camps for fear of retribution or death. When the inciters of the genocide peeled themselves away from the camps, thousands of refugees who had wanted to return to their home provinces for months were free to cross the border.

International organizations saw the potential movements as a way to gain visibility and access to new resources. But the new government in Rwanda had worked closely with the international community, building capacity to address the initial needs of any returns. Water points and transit centers, key elements of a well-organized and coordinated return, had been pre-arranged by the government. The role of the international community would be to provide the refugees with health care, education, and shelter in their home provinces upon their return.

International organizations took the opportunity to seize the media spotlight. I was instructed to be at the border wearing a T-shirt and a cap embossed with the organization's logo. But the initial preparations that had been organized by the government of Rwanda had been confirmed by the media. Christiane Amanpour, the international correspondent for CNN, had come and gone—a sure indicator that any additional international media attention would quickly wane.

Home office staff did not respect the input of senior staff on the ground, making decisions in isolation without a clear understanding of the context. Emergency experts descended upon Kigali—often unannounced—to manage the return at the border, even though they had been informed that the initial stages of the anticipated return were being capably organized by the Government of Rwanda.

Hotel rooms in Kigali were sparse. A network news crew from the US wanted to do a segment on child soldiers. I was asked to host a team from the network in my small house. I agreed, with the understanding that we did not work with child soldiers, and if we said that we did, we would be banned from continuing with our current work in the country.

The staff member who headed up our small emergency response team arranged to fly to Kigali. I was instructed to organize a convoy to get him to the border as soon he landed. Staff on the ground worked frantically to receive the influx of their international colleagues as international organizations tumbled into Kigali.

As a number of international organizations clamored to welcome the refugees as they crossed over the border, Assumpta quietly passed. A memorial service was organized at a Catholic church in Kigali. Immediately following the service, I needed to drive out to the airport to pick up my colleague.

When I arrived at the church, there was standing room only. Someone at the entrance motioned me to follow him. He walked to the center of the church, depositing me in the pew directly in front of the diamond-shaped altar. I looked around. I was the only foreigner in the crowded church.

The mourners stood holding their arms loosely in front of them, enveloping their grief. Their faces sullen, their eyes would remain dry as I, who was immediately overwhelmed with emotion, began to sob uncontrollably. While no one else in the church cried, I stood gasping for air. The tears flowed so freely I gave up trying to hold them back. For over a year I had maintained my composure as people around me were falling apart, but I could no longer deny my unfathomable grief.

I left the church and drove to the airport. My colleague deplaned ready to hit the ground running. It was ten o'clock at night when I briefed him on the situation and updated him on the arrangements that I had made for his trip to the border the following day. I told him that I had just come from a memorial service, but he was not interested. He wanted more details on the logistics and donor environment, which I dutifully provided.

When we arrived at my house, I showed him to the guest room. Shortly afterward, he came out into the main room to inform me that one of the legs on his bed had broken. He wanted it repaired immediately. I told him that I didn't have the necessary tools to repair it, and being so late in the night, I was not able to call a logistician due to the security situation. It would be too dangerous to ask one of our national staff to travel into the city at night. Disgruntled, he retreated to his room.

Other colleagues from the home office had arrived days earlier. I worked with them to conduct assessments and write proposals to obtain new funding for expanded activities as a result of the anticipated returns. Although I had enjoyed open and mutually supportive professional relationships with them in the past, word got back to me that one colleague had informed the home office that I had not supported her. I didn't understand the rift between us. I had explained to my colleagues that my assistant, who normally worked closely with me to arrange and manage international visits, had recently died.

Early the next morning, the home office team left for the border in their logo-clad T-shirts and caps. The following day, they returned to Kigali after finding that there was no need for them to stay. The anticipated movements had yet to begin, and they had confirmed the capacity of the government of Rwanda to manage the initial stages of the return. They informed me that any substantial role for our organization would need to wait until the populations returned to their home provinces. We agreed that I would continue to monitor potential funding opportunities as the situation unfolded. The emergency team left Kigali the next day.

I was on the verge of resignation, but I soldiered on. Within weeks, however, I was told that the home office was sending in a stringer to manage where I had failed, even though we did not have any serious management issues on the ground. I understood their disdain for me. I had been easy to get along with when I had joined the organization. The trauma that surrounded my work, however, had deeply affected me. I had changed. I had had little experience or training to effectively cope in such a difficult environment. Exhausted, I poured the little remaining energy that I possessed into supporting my national staff. Almost nothing was left to develop and maintain necessary relationships with the home office. I was expected to communicate broadly, and regularly, across departments, but I was not successful. My standing in the organization faltered.

One month remained on my contract. I was offered, and accepted a transfer to work in a neighboring country through the end of my contract. If I refused the offer, there were no other options for me to stay with the organization. A few weeks earlier, a close friend had asked me why I had never considered leaving, even though my situation was so dire. I had replied that I had made a commitment. More importantly, I did not want to leave the national staff so soon after Assumpta had died, but I no longer had a choice.

The day of my departure, Suleiman escorted me to the airport. As I prepared to leave with my luggage, the stringer that the home office had brought in to replace me was positioned, arms folded, on the stairway in front of the office, watching as I descended the stairs.

Earlier that week, she had cited me for not refreshing the emergency fuel that we held in underground tanks in the rear of the office compound. As I was departing for the airport with the head of logistics, she ordered the staff to change the fuel, even though there would not be anyone there to supervise the task. Her first directive was left to anyone in earshot.

I climbed into the white Land Cruiser. Through the window, I saw a plethora of garden hoses snaking out from under the outside fencing surrounding the underground fuel reserve. As the hoses dropped into the newly opened tanks, the woman from headquarters entered the office. I pulled the door of the truck shut and dropped my head. The sweat and toil I had invested in my work over the past year and a half had been rolled back in an instant. As I drove away from the office compound for the last time, it was as if my own blood were being siphoned.

As Suleiman and I approached the security checkpoint, I stopped. Once my luggage had passed through security, I would need to pass through the gate and collect my bags on the other side. Suleiman would not be able to accompany me any further.

I picked up the smallest bag and placed it on the conveyor belt. I slowly bent over to pick up the other bag. Lifting it, I rested it on the edge of the machine, balancing it heavily against my body. As I released it from my grasp, I watched as the bag was swallowed into the X-ray machine. The rubber flaps slapped against the side of the bag, edging it deeper into the darkness. After it had disappeared into the belly of the machine, I twisted around to face Suleiman.

"Thank you for coming with me today," I said.

It was then that Suleiman reached out his arms to grab onto my elbows. In return, as naturally as if I had practiced the greeting every day of my life, I reached out and grabbed onto his—cradling them gently in my palms, savoring the intimacy of the moment.

"Thank you so much for staying with me," I said. "I respect you so much for your courage."

Then, as if on cue, we dropped each other's elbows and I turned to walk away. I crossed through the security gate to collect my bags, fumbling with them aimlessly—not wanting to look back. With my luggage in tow, I turned to see Suleiman standing in the same spot where I had left him. I smiled and waved. He stood stoically, watching until I disappeared behind the departure gate in front of me.

NOTES ON

Suleiman's Return

Back in Minneapolis, I stumbled on an opening at the Center for Victims of Torture. I applied. After being asked to interview, I thought of Suleiman, and the memories of his arrest and subsequent beatings began to haunt me. I had not had the energy or time to work through some of my own traumatic experiences when I was on the ground in Rwanda. Once home, when I no longer had the constant barrage of pressing responsibilities cluttering my mind, I began to write. The following piece recounts the day that Suleiman returned to work after having been arrested and jailed for over a month without charges.

SULEIMAN'S RETURN

Suleiman shuffled into my office. Although I had not heard him, I felt his presence. I turned and smiled. He stood tall, although he was a stout man. One month had passed since his arrest.

"How are you?" I asked.

I had been told not to visit, my presence would most certainly worsen the beatings. Each day we had sent someone from the staff with food, so we knew that he had not been transferred from the jail to the prison.

"I've come back to work," he said.

"But, how do you feel?" I asked.

He turned his face away from me.

"I have a headache," he whispered.

I stared at him blankly. Turning, I reached for my purse. I pulled out a small pill case and emptied the contents into my hand. I offered the pills to him, and he extended his hand, but he did not move closer to me to take them. I stood up, stepping toward him to deposit the pills into his open palm.

"Go home," I said. "Go home and rest no matter how long it takes. Come back when you feel better."

The words *thank you* fell quietly from his lips.

As I stood watching, he turned and slowly shuffled out of the room. Once he was out of sight, I closed the door, leaned over, and grabbed my gut.

There was nothing that I could do to soften the blows, nothing, to ease the concussion. It was too late to wipe the blood that had flowed out of Suleiman's ears.

NOTES ON

Thy Neighbor's Heart

I wrote this sonnet in twenty minutes. It surprised me how easily the words flowed from my pen. Unlike the process I used to write my other sonnets, I only revised it slightly. The verse is not beautiful. The cadence is rapt with dissonance; the meter is flawed. Two lines are missing beats. In the second line of the first quatrain, the missing beat hangs after the word *retreating*. In the first line of the third quatrain, the laugh of children, usually lighthearted, is harrowing.

Yet, with all of its machinations, I love to read this sonnet because it brings me relief. It allows me to spit out the ugliness of the genocide as it connects me to my own heartbeat after the quiet reprieve prior to the couplet.

"Thy Neighbor's Heart" depicts the role of the humanitarian aid agencies during the initial emergency response after the genocide in Rwanda. The day that I visited the women's prison ward with my program director informed the turn at the volta, line nine of the sonnet.

THY NEIGHBOR'S HEART

The beauty of the sunlight leaves my eyes
As does the midnight moon—retreating
Wide-eyed children knock stars down from the sky
With thy neighbor's heart, which has stopped beating.
After the shots had rung-out through the night,
The convoys arrived without incident—
Truckloads of rightful wares to ease the plight
Of a million plus souls, with prayers, were sent.
Thy neighbor has seen how life can laugh
In the faces of children wielding sticks
And stones—war waged by angels on behalf
Of their mothers, whose spirits like…clocks…tick…
Justice lies dormant while souls stand pleading,
With thy neighbor's heart, which has stopped beating.

Minneapolis, Minnesota, 1997

Chapter Five

FIRST FORAY HOME

Minneapolis 1997–98

I sat for hours, staring out the front window. I jumped nervously over small water-main covers on the side of the road—mistaking them for anti-personnel landmines. In time, I regained some of my energy and verve for life. But, it was less intense than before I had departed for Kigali.

Working with a grief counselor, I bounced between traumatic memories of the past and broken hopes for the future. I was irritable without cause. The suffering I had experienced and observed in Rwanda had been deeply embedded within me. I had steeled myself too well.

I had not lived with or near my parents for over fifteen years. When I returned from Rwanda, I was on my way to Florida with hopes of getting married. But instead of gaining a husband, I gained two best friends when my parents and I became roommates.

Most mornings, I sat with my father over breakfast. One day, as he was buttering his toast, he put his knife down and looked at me from across the table. "Did you see the cover of *Modern Maturity* this month?" he asked.

I had not. Nor had I seen the publication in the house.

"Next month," he said, "when your adult child returns."

After raising eight children, my parents had hit their rhythm again as a couple. I had only arranged to stay with them for a few weeks. Two weeks quickly morphed into a year. When they decided to move out of state, I was evicted, but not before spending a number of long, leisurely days with my father.

We lived near a lake. A paved walkway through densely wooded areas snaked around it. Small creeks edged out of the main body of water. Fuzzy cattails blew pollen onto the air around us as we passed by.

"You were always a rebel," my father said.

I looked over at him, confused. We continued walking. A man and a woman, out for a stroll, were approaching us on the walkway.

"Howdy," he said. "How're you doing?"

No response.

My father tutored me in common courtesy. "It's best to greet everyone," he said, "even if they don't greet you back—like those clowns. I'm not going to let them get me down."

I told my father that I had decided to see a counselor.

"What do you need to do that for?" he asked.

"I'm so irritable, Dad," I explained. "You see how I'm taking it out on Mom. It's not fair. That's why."

Whether he understood or not, I never knew. We never spoke of it again. Instead, he showed his support through his greetings whenever I would return from a session.

I fell ill. My mother drove me to the clinic, where I sat with her for hours with a sharp pain on the left side of my abdomen and no diagnosis. The nurse escorted us back into the examination room.

"She was in Africa," my mother told the nurse.

I was referred to the emergency room of the nearby hospital. "She was in Africa," my mother said to the emergency room doctor.

Her statements did nothing, however, to aid in the diagnosis. In the evening, after a bevy of tests, an ultrasound unearthed a blockage in my abdomen. The emergency room doctor recommended an appendectomy.

"There are risks if we don't take it out," the doctor said. "If it bursts, you may not be able to have children."

I looked over at my mother.

"Take it out," I said.

I signed the release form, even though my symptoms were not presenting normally—the blockage was on the wrong side.

A year later, I was in Washington, DC to attend a day of back-to-back meetings before flying out to Senegal on a short-term consulting job. I had had a cup of coffee before leaving the hotel that day, but my schedule had been too full to take a break to eat. After my meetings, I met my friends Kitty and Tom for drinks.

Tom ordered a bulb of roasted elephant garlic. I squeezed the warm, soft insides out of a clove and smoothed it over a piece of crusty French bread. I popped the morsel into my mouth and washed it down with some wine. The garlic was creamy and tart. We ordered another bulb. Although I hadn't eaten anything since the day before, I was too tired to join my friends for dinner. I went back to the hotel to prepare for my overseas departure the next day.

Later that evening, while I was working at the hotel, I wasn't able to sit comfortably. I went into the bathroom where I experienced a sensation that I had never experienced before. I stood up and looked down. In the bowl, a translucent coil was unfolding. There was nothing else around it. The coil became a spring. The spring became an iridescent rope over eight inches long. As I stood watching, one of the rope ends reached out of the water.

"Shit!" I screamed. "Shit!"

A live worm floated in the toilet bowl below. I left the bathroom in search of a container to transport it to the emergency room at the hospital. It was late in the evening. There would be gunshot wounds and other more pressing emergencies that would be triaged ahead of me. If I presented a long, pink worm in a plastic bag—as offspring—I risked being detained in a sister facility. If this happened, I would be prevented from catching my flight out of the US the next day. Instead of calling a cab, I flushed the toilet.

I called Kitty and woke her. She passed on the number of a friend and former Peace Corps volunteer who had recently become a doctor. He diagnosed me immediately, telling me that his brother also had had the ailment some years earlier. He phoned a prescription into a nearby pharmacy that I picked up the next morning on my way to the airport.

The treatment for ascaris—one of six infections in the roundworm family—is one 500-milligram tablet of mebendazole, trade name Vermox. The second option, my preferred treatment, is a blister pack of six 100-milligram tablets, taken twice daily for three consecutive days. Both options are extremely effective, with little or no side effects as they inhibit the glucose uptake in the parasites, immobilizing them. Once perished, the parasites pass though the stools. The first time I contracted ascaris, I had inadvertently relied on a homeopathic remedy—the sulfur of the elephant garlic had shooed the worm out of my system. The infection, which I could have had for up to two years, most likely had included more worms. These parasites were ushered out of my system over the following days by Vermox.

Throughout Africa, the treatment for roundworm costs no more than the equivalent of two US dollars. In New York City, I once bought the drug for forty-five dollars. In Minneapolis, I had been offered and had agreed to have an appendectomy. After the surgery, the doctor had assured me that my appendix had been ready to burst. I did not have a follow-up visit with him a year later, however, to tell him that I also had had a worm.

CROSSING TO SAFETY

It just stopped.

It just stopped—like a heart
That stopped beating.

As I sat by my window
Shots rang out.

Perhaps it was merely
A truck—toddling
Down the rocky hillside.

Excitement mounted,
As did reservations—
And once I crossed to safety
The wheels of the truck
Came to a screeching halt.

And, it just stopped.

Minneapolis, Minnesota, 1997

NOTES ON

Second Trilogy

The story in this sonnet is depicted in a sonnet cycle and tells of a love affair that stretched over many years. It started when I was eighteen years old—the summer Elvis died. It ended and was rekindled more than eighteen years later, when I was living in Rwanda.

Following my graduation from high school, I traveled with a friend to a small town in North Dakota, where we stayed with her relatives during an extended summer vacation. It was during that summer that I met Kevin.

Kevin had only been in North Dakota for a short time—having moved there a few years earlier with his father, who had been relocated to plant missiles in silos on the surrounding farms. After completing his work, his father returned to Florida. Kevin loved the people, weather, and lifestyle in North Dakota so much that he stayed on as a hired hand, harvesting wheat after his father left.

I went out to the wheat field to greet Kevin during that first summer. He had a huge afro, large-framed glasses, and steely blue eyes. He was shirtless. Chaff from the wheat he was combining dusted his sweaty skin.

I climbed up the side of the combine and handed him a plastic sandwich bag with a can of Coca-Cola nestled in ice cubes. The ice cubes had begun to melt. He pulled out the soda and poured the water from the melted ice over his head.

Laughing, I jumped off of the side of the combine and ran across the wheat field. When I reached the car, I smiled and waved. Kevin nodded, put the combine in gear, and continued fluttering through the field.

Years later, when I was working in Rwanda, Kevin called me. We had only one international telephone line, located at the reception desk on the first floor. My assistant came into my office to tell me that I had an international call. I bolted down the steps, clanking in my wooden clogs, holding the folds of my calf-length skirt as I ran to grab the phone.

"Hello?"

"Do you know who this is?" a male voice asked.

I spun through the Rolodex of my mind, flipping through my time in Washington, DC, the years I had spent in the Peace Corps. I couldn't place the voice. I went further back in time.

"I know who you are!" I exclaimed. "What are you doing calling me? Are you going to turn forty soon and are calling everyone in your little black book who wouldn't sleep with you when they were eighteen years old?"

"Precisely," he said.

Kevin was the funniest person I had ever met. I sent him messages describing thousands of people accused of genocide, crammed into prisons barefoot with standing room only. He responded that it was a normal day in central Florida, sunny and humid, with hundreds of older folks sporting white, patent leather shoes. The contrast between our daily lives was stark, but these exchanges brought some much-needed levity to my life.

When Kevin reappeared in my life, he was a welcome distraction. I fell in love, but it was not meant to be. Still, it took many years until I was fully able to let him go.

Writing "Second Trilogy," helped me to work through some of the more confusing elements of my broken relationship. I chose three phrases to outline the story. Each phrase had fourteen letters that I placed vertically, creating a framework for a sonnet cycle. Each line had a pre-set starting point, allowing me to explore many options as I drafted and redrafted the lines of each stanza. I added a couplet to each sonnet in the cycle and, once completed, slipped the sonnets into a drawer with the others. Free of any anger or frustration that I may have harbored in the past, I finally was able to move on with my life.

SECOND TRILOGY

I. Unrequited Love
Unfounded, lonely lovers scheme
Neither right nor wrong, but two thieves
Reminisce not through fitful dreams
Entre deux the other believes.
Quintessentially life confessed
Utterances prodding my mind,
Injurious are deeds professed
Tempered words are gifts in kind.
Enough of endings, no more sighs
Daunting prospects are left to chance
Licentiousness of days gone by,
Obstinate befuddled romance.
Velvet is the feel of my heart,
Errant pile once thrust apart.

II. On Seeing it is So
Ominous were the signs of fall
Nemesis thine own eyes beget
Seductive unraveling stalled,
Endlessly pleading no regret.
Elucidation, steel-blue eyes
Intimacy, abandoned hope
Nebulousness did not disguise,

Guttural were my means to cope.
Instead of moving on, I stayed
Transfixed beneath the empty skies
Inherently overextended delayed,
Seldom heard are nature's sighs.
Soundlessly, the leaves left the trees,
Of little consequence, I see.

III. Belief in Myself
Bereft no more the clouds are gone
Exuberance flows throughout each vein
Lingering buds greet me at dawn
Iridescent waves cleanse the pain.
Effervescent skin dons a smile
Fundamentally I begin
Interlinear thoughts beguile
Native sons are gathered within.
Many years will pass by my side
Yearning, I will remember youth
Such fears I no longer abide,
Elusiveness pales not the truth.
Love is what remains of my voice
Forgiveness graces future choice.

Minneapolis, Minnesota, 1998

SERBIA

0 ⊢━━━━━━━━━━━ 80 km
0 ⊢━━━━━━━━━━━ 40 miles

Chapter Six

BLACK NIGHT WHITE ANGEL

Belgrade 1998–99

I arrived in Belgrade in the summer of 1998, the week that the US embassies in Kenya and Tanzania were bombed. I watched from my hotel room as emergency personnel grappled with the carnage. I had recently worked in the region and knew people stationed in or near the embassies in both countries.

I had been waiting to be deployed to Botswana, a peaceful country in southern Africa, but I had landed in Belgrade instead. A former director had suggested that I go there. Because I knew and respected her, I agreed to work with her again. I was the director of a training program funded by the US government. I had three staff. Two were of Montenegrin decent and one was of Croatian descent. All three of them, however, had spent their early years in Belgrade and considered themselves Yugoslavs.

I was welcomed with a dinner in a traditional restaurant on a cobbled street in the old district of the city. Platters of grilled meat filled the table, crowding out small, crystal goblets of plum brandy, sipped before and during dinner. There were no vegetables. In future weeks, I would chance upon a *paradajz* salad, only to be served a plate of sliced tomatoes. In Serbia, I was told, meat was a vegetable.

When my colleague Vanja and I met with her friends, the conversation inevitably reached back centuries, ending with heated debates of the 1389 Battle of Kosovo. Cigarettes—two packs each—stacked beside bottles of homemade plum brandy graced the table in front of us when we met at each other's homes. Large, cold beers from SKS, the student union on the main boulevard in central Belgrade, were shared among us like bottles of wine when we ventured out.

When I was alone, it was difficult to read street signs; the language was written in Cyrillic. I found a language class and began to study Serbian. Each morning following my class, I spoke to my colleagues in their native tongue, spitting out the new words that I had learned the night before. They laughed and corrected my pronunciation. They taught me profanities—a regular feature of the language spoken by the younger generation. I was not put off by the obscene language; my friends and colleagues in Serbia had soft hearts. Many were poets. If they did not write poetry, they read it. I felt at home with my new friends—I fit in.

I learned the Cyrillic alphabet and collected humorous phrases in a notebook. I took my first exam, surprised that I was able to read the questions written in Cyrillic. After the exam, my teacher provided me with thirteen new verbs. The political situation intervened, however, before I was able to learn how to conjugate them.

Relations with the West were strained. There were also internal tensions following the war in Bosnia, especially among colleagues and former friends—many having fought on opposite sides of the war. Politics found its way into every conversation before ending in a heated argument.

I lived in Belgrade for eight months. During this time I was evacuated three times, only to return twice. The first time I was evacuated, my colleagues were more concerned for my safety than for their own. I was the only expatriate working as a US government contractor with my organization in Belgrade. Yet, I was not allowed to join the road convey organized by the US government to Budapest.

My Serbian friends were aghast that the US government would leave me behind to fend for myself, especially since there were so few Americans working in Belgrade. It was difficult to explain to my colleagues that the US government made a clear distinction between official US government employees and Americans, or others, who worked for international organizations as sub-contractors with US government funds.

When I called the airlines, there was only one seat left in business class—on Austrian Airlines. I was not permitted to fly business class without authorization from the US government. I explained my situation to the ticket agent. The following day, Austrian Airlines offered to sell me the last business-class seat at the economy fare.

Each time I was evacuated, I remained at the evacuation point for fifteen days. During this time, the US government employed diplomacy with the government of Serbia. After fifteen days, I returned to Belgrade with the other US government employees and contractors. For months, negotiations went back and forth.

The second time I was evacuated, I was equally concerned about my staff and myself. Following complaints from US government contractors who were not allowed to join the road convoy during the first evacuation, an invitation was extended to contractors during the second evacuation. I didn't have a car. I was offered a ride by another international organization, but I was told that I could not bring any luggage. For a second time, I flew from Belgrade to Budapest.

I was cautioned by the US government administrative officer not to return to Belgrade. Negotiations were not going well. The political situation was increasingly tense. But I needed to go back. My staff did not have sufficient funds for living expenses. If there was a further breakdown in political relations, they would need cash to survive.

I was worried that I would be stopped and searched at the airport. If airport officials found the cash I was carrying, they would surely confiscate it. More alarming, I could be beaten. I rolled the cash into a small bundle and secured it tightly under my waistband. My plane landed. As I moved through the airport toward customs, I felt as if all eyes were upon me. Although I did not look differently from the others, it seemed as if everyone knew I was American.

I kept my passport pressed close to my chest so that no one could see the blue cover. As I neared the immigration booth, I began to sweat slightly. When I was in front of the window, I slipped my passport under the glass.

"Dobar Dan!" Good morning, said the immigration official with a big smile. "You are welcome in Belgrade!"

I stepped back, faltering slightly. After I passed through immigration, I found my colleague waiting for me outside on the curb. We greeted each other warmly before crossing the street toward the parking lot. We loaded my luggage into the back of his small car and drove to the office. I pulled out a bottle and poured out four small glasses of *Palinka*, Hungarian peach brandy. We toasted to my return.

"What happened?" I asked. "I thought that I'd be searched and beaten when I passed through immigration, but I was welcomed with open arms."

Vanja laughed.

"Of course they welcomed you with open arms," she said. "You are American, and all of the other Americans are evacuating. If you are coming into the country with your American passport, it means that it will be a few more days before the bombing begins, so everyone was happy to see you!"

A few days later, I was evacuated from Belgrade for the third, and final, time. Before I left, I was more concerned about the welfare of my colleagues than for myself. As I prepared to depart, I asked Vanja to tape the wall safe open. I didn't want there to be any confusion if the secret police raided our office.

Working for an American organization had put my staff at risk. They had surely been followed, and their neighbors had most likely been asked to report on their every movement as my neighbors had been asked to report on mine. Every time that I returned to my apartment, as the old elevator door creaked open, so did the thick, old door of my neighbor's apartment across the hall.

An old woman or her son—if he wasn't out selling used books on the main boulevard—peered at me suspiciously each time I stepped out of the elevator. Then, as suddenly as the door had opened, it slammed shut, leaving my unrequited greeting to dissipate in the dark, musty hallway.

My office was in a three-story building on a main boulevard opposite an underpass. The exhaust from the vehicles below wafted into the windows in spurts of black mist. The outside walls of the building harbored a layer of dark, greasy soot that had grown thick over the years. My organization occupied the bottom floor of the building. Each morning as I entered the building, I passed under an assault rifle that had been tastefully painted on the glass divider over the tall, wooden doorway. The sign was used to entice clients to the second floor. The top floor of the building was leased by the US-based International Republican Institute, another American-based organization working to support the development of the civil society in Belgrade.

To kill time on weekends, I took long walks along the main boulevard. On one occasion, my shadow was obvious. There was no one else on the street other than the two of us. Yet, he kept a safe distance. When I stopped, he stopped, perusing the contents behind shop windows. When I crossed the street, he crossed the street. He was a handsome man, and I would have preferred if he had walked beside me. I gladly would have welcomed the company. But he kept his distance. When I entered my apartment building, he slipped away.

I arrived with a six-month visa. Once expired, it was necessary to renew it on a monthly basis. When I went to the Ministry of the Interior to extend my visa, I was accompanied by another international colleague. It was eight o'clock in the morning.

We had been waiting for over an hour when the door to the immigration official's office opened. I was invited to enter; my colleague was told to wait. The young, attractive immigration official motioned me to sit. A lit cigarette hung slightly off to the side of his mouth, his unshaven face ruggedly pricking out from behind the smoke. The list of questions began.

How long had I been in Belgrade? Where did I like to drink? What didn't I like about his country? I told him the length of my stay and that I liked to drink beer at SKS, the student union.

"How many beers do you drink?" he asked.

I told him that I drank two big beers, often sharing them with my colleagues.

"I drink sixteen!" he bristled, sitting up proudly.

Judging from his appearance, I believed him. When responding to his question about what I did not like about his country, I told him that I did not like the pollution that wafted from the cars as they entered the tunnel below my office window.

"Is that all?" he asked. "What else don't you like about my country?"

"Nothing else," I replied.

The young man continued to interrogate me on my daily activities. I suspected that he was working to corroborate any other reports that may have been submitted by my neighbors or others. When he was finished, he made a few notes in a file and placed it in the cupboard at the rear corner of his office. He asked me to wait outside of his office while he spoke to my colleague.

The office door opened, and the young immigration official appeared through the threshold.

"Now that we are finished, it is time to drink!" he said.

It was ten in the morning. The young man signaled me to join him before turning back toward the interior of his office. I entered the office and sat down. My colleague was asked what he wanted to drink.

"A Coke, please," he said.

The immigration official turned to me.

"What would you like?"

I knew that it was customary to have plum brandy with coffee in the morning. I didn't particularly like Coca-Cola, so I opted to follow the cultural norm.

"Slivu!" I replied, with exuberance.

My colleague glared over at me confusedly.

"Good choice!" my host shot back.

We drank quickly, thanked the immigration official, and rose to leave. Although we did not know it then, we were never to return. The following month, my colleague and I were both evacuated from Belgrade for the third time. When the bombing began, a missile traveled down the main boulevard before striking its target, successfully zeroing in upon and demolishing the Serbian Ministry of the Interior.

In the build-up to the bombing, teachers had been instructed to inform their students that World War II carpet bombing techniques—which had desecrated the homes of their grandparents—would again be utilized by the West. The messages frightened children and parents alike. Calming the fears of my friends and colleagues, I informed them that I had seen newer bombing techniques on television in the West during the first war in Iraq. Updated bombing techniques, I had said, could allow a missile to travel down the boulevard and turn left based on a pre-programmed command. The techniques used to instill fear in the population by the Serbian government, I had added, were outdated.

Following the hit on the Ministry of the Interior, the premises were searched. A large safe in the basement of the building had withstood the blast. Stacked inside of the safe lay six hundred kilograms of heroin—1,320 pounds. My visa extension file, which had been tucked into a cupboard on the second floor of the building, however, was presumably lost forever.

To reclaim lost territory, a twentieth-century chapter to the story of 1389 was written in an arrogant display of aggression by Serbia's president. With the bombing came the forcible exile of vast numbers of ethnic Albanians who had been living beside Serbians in Kosovo for centuries.

To stem the flow of displaced ethnic Albanians, NATO retaliated. But initial efforts by NATO did not stop the massive exodus out of Kosovo as residents were loaded onto trains and sent south to Albania. Equally, citizens in Belgrade were loaded onto buses by the government at nightfall, transported to bridges along the river, and served up as human shields.

The residents of Belgrade hovered in the basements of schoolhouses and other public buildings for weeks. Large replicas of the White Angel fresco, that had shielded the monastery from aggression for centuries, were employed by the people as spiritual armor.

In Belgrade, the Chinese embassy took a hit. My Serbian friends had expected what everyone else in the world had not. Inside the borders of Serbia, at least one local journalist had reported that the basement of the Chinese embassy was providing refuge to high-level government officials, including President Miloševic and his wife.

Only one other widely reported account of an errant bomb had circulated widely in the international press. But unlike the bomb that had landed squarely on the Chinese embassy, the second errant missile lodged over the border in neighboring Bulgaria in the middle of a deserted field.

NOTES ON

Spark at Mileševo

I was invited on a day trip by a group of Americans to travel outside of Belgrade to visit the Church of the Ascension, one of the many monasteries in the southwest of Serbia. It is home to *The Angel at Christ's Tomb*, a fresco more popularly known as The White Angel, a masterpiece in Serbian Medieval painting. My colleagues asked me to take pictures of the fresco during my visit. I told them that I was a poet, preferring to capture my impressions in verse.

Following my visit to Mileševo, I began working on a sonnet, but I was not able to write a couplet to complete the poem. I worked on the piece for weeks, searching for an ending. One night, as I sat in bed writing, I changed the structure of the poem by expanding it to include five stanzas. I wrote of the centuries-old conflict in Mileševo. I described earth's rumblings as flesh severed bone to depict the hundreds of battles waged outside the walls of the monastery. In the final lines, I wrote of the contrast between outer conflict and inner peace.

Finally the poem was complete. I closed my notebook and lay down to sleep. Less than an hour later, an earthquake shook the foundation of the concrete building below me. I jumped up, grabbed a sweater, and ran out into the hallway. My neighbor and her son were scrambling into the elevator as I opened the door. When they saw me, they quickly slammed the steel gate of the elevator shut.

I took the stairs down to the third level and knocked on the door of the apartment directly below mine. An old woman peered out from behind the portal. I asked her if I could use her phone. Without speaking, she outstretched an index finger and pulled back a knotted knuckle, signaling me to enter.

Crossing the threshold, time rolled back more than fifty years. A black, rotary-dial telephone anchored the top of an elaborately carved side table. Large lace doilies were draped over the back of the sofa and the thick, protruding armrests of the chairs throughout the room. Sheets placed on the sofa to make a bed had been thrust back in haste.

I dialed the number to the US embassy. The marine guard answered. I said that there had been an earthquake. I asked him what I should do. "Stay put, ma'am," was the only reply.

I thanked him and moved to return the earpiece to the cradle of the old phone. The apparatus slipped out of my fingers, loudly knocking the round finger-dialer. I recovered my grip, replacing the earpiece securely. Thanking my neighbor, I retreated to my apartment above.

The next day, I noticed that the Juliet balcony on the second floor of the building next to my office had fallen. The only discernible destruction from the previous night's rumblings had landed in the precise place on the sidewalk where the one-legged man stood each day soliciting handouts from passersby. Armpits perched upon metal crutches, hand extended, he had needed to shift his position on the sidewalk slightly after the earthquake.

I pulled off the top of my small Tupperware keychain and emptied the contents into the man's outstretched hand. My colleagues had told me that no one paid bus fare. If I were asked, I was told to place the correct coinage for the ticket in the conductor's palm without comment. On days that I wasn't approached by the conductor, the coins tumbled into the palm of the one-legged sentry standing guard at the entrance to my office.

Earlier that fall, Vanja suggested that I publish my poem, "Spark at Mileševo," in a local literary journal edited by one of her friends. I worked with my colleagues, Mosha and Natasha, to translate the poem for the publication. Natasha provided the direct translation. Mosha prepared the *prepev,* or literary translation. Mosha was a brilliant poet and writer. I could not understand the translation, but I had no doubt that he had used his native language to deepen the meaning of the original poetic underpinnings of the piece.

My colleagues and I made a holiday card out of the poem, placing a replica of the White Angel fresco on the cover of the card. The history of the fresco was noted on the back of the card. Printed on the inside left page of the card was the poem, and on the right side, embossed in gold lettering, was the message: PEACE EXISTS.

We sent the card to friends and colleagues in the region. Following a conflict concerning the management of the shared space in the entryway of the office building, in a bid of reconciliation, we sent a signed card to the office on the second floor. The weapons dealer responded in kind, sending down a large wall calendar with a picture of a vulture sitting atop a distant mountain, preparing to strike out at an unidentified target below. He also sent a pen, embossed with the word "Sniper."

The conflict over the shared space in the entryway continued. For a second time, the weapons dealer stripped our brass organizational mailbox plate off the wall—it was not uniform with the others. Impulsively, I went up the stairs to the second floor to discuss the matter face-to-face. My colleague followed me up the stairs to translate. I knocked on the thick wood door and was invited into the reception area. I quickly realized that the kind-looking man with the large blue eyes, whom I had passed in the hallway on occasion, was not the weapons dealer.

The door to the weapons dealer's office opened and I was greeted by small, dark, squinting eyes protruding out of a short, round, angry body. As soon as he saw me, the man began yelling. As I backed out of the reception area into the hallway, I told my colleague to say that I was sorry. My colleague stood courteously as the man continued hurdling insults in Serbian. I turned and slipped out of the door. My colleague followed me into the hallway.

The weapons dealer reached his head out into the hallway as we descended the stairs. His final insult was lobbed down the stairs in English. "Fuck you! And fuck Monica Lewinsky!" he roared. As I reached the doorway in front of my office below, the office door above me slammed shut.

A few weeks earlier, a national newspaper had published the results of a poll on local attitudes toward the US president. President William Jefferson Clinton was a good politician, the citizens had said, but he was a better lover.

Following my visit to his office that day, it was clear that the weapons dealer had not seen the holiday card with the White Angel fresco that I had sent him. The kindhearted, Serbian man with the large blue eyes had sent me the gifts. The big boss hated Americans.

SPARK AT MILEŠEVO

With an outstretched arm gilded gold
An eternal flame through the years
Perched above armies, stories told
Of faith, of a white knight unseared.

He who has loved shall always know
The pain of loss within fists clenched
As warm as a blanket of snow
Possession precedes, then is wrenched

From grasp. Is this as it should be?
For centuries the flint-blistered stone
Withstood the mounting seas—
Earth's rumblings as flesh severed bone.

Dare not defy the life-giving veins
That flow between heart and thought.
Heed not that which shelters rain
Nor take refuge where none is sought.

It was not man's but nature's spark,
Igniting Mileševo fields
From outside armies bore their mark
From inside the white angel shields.

Belgrade, Serbia (Former Yugoslavia), 1998

NOTES ON

A Tear from Heaven

Aleksa was a close friend of my colleague, Vanja. In time, I would meet many of Vanja's friends—artists, journalists, musicians, former colleagues, and schoolmates, but we spent my initial weeks in Belgrade with Aleksa. It was early winter when Aleksa prepared to depart for his first skiing trip of the season. We said our good-byes. But news came back to us before he did that he had tumbled head-on into a tree while skiing. In an instant, he was gone.

The wake was held at the cemetery. As rain fell, I took my place at the end of a long line of mourners. Inside the cement building, candles were the only source of light. Aleksa's former wife, Dragana, gasped when she saw me. "Thank you for coming," she said as renewed tears flowed down her face. "The last time that I saw Aleksa was at your party."

A few weeks earlier, I had hosted a party in my apartment in downtown Belgrade. Both Aleksa and Dragana had come, staying late into the night, leaving with the others once all of the plum brandy had been emptied from its homemade casks.

It was the first and last party that I hosted in Belgrade.

A TEAR FROM HEAVEN

A raindrop fell
Onto my eye—
A tear from heaven.

From out of the shadows
I mounted the stairs,
Chiseled, uneven.

Snow on the mountains,
Life in the balance,
More than one can bear.

In the cathedral,
Faces of icons,
Life beyond compare.

Finale: Allegro,
Dancing with angels,
Stumbling on our knees.

Raise the gold chalice,
Four silver teardrops,
Languish on the breeze.

Belgrade, Serbia (Former Yugoslavia), 1999

THE PROMISE OF PEACE

The blast threw me off of my feet.
As I rose, you fell to your knees.
My blood burns like flames on the street.
Shards of glass blind my eyes but I see.
Extended hand lay down your arms,
Three winters, four springs have gone by.
River of life spit out your charms,
Wash the tears that I no longer cry.
Fresh fallen snow covers torn leaves,
Moss weaves a carpet of fleece,
Smooth rounded stones, symphonic reprieve
From the source flows the promise of peace.
Voices call out: "The current is strong!"
Fill my lungs, Sarajevo, with song.

Sarajevo, Bosnia and Herzegovina (Former Yugoslavia), 1999

NOTES ON

Blind Return

In the aftermath of the bombing, I returned to the city where I had taken up temporary residence the year before. It was during this visit that I wrote the sonnet "Blind Return." Prior to settling into the popular central café on the main boulevard to write, I strolled down the side street where my former office had been located.

As I neared the entryway to the building, my eyes fell upon a man leaning against the cement wall, his head shaded by the Juliet balcony above him. His arms, draped securely on the top of his crutches, hung loosely at his sides. As I approached him, I grabbed his outstretched hand. We expressed a warm greeting to each other through our eyes. After a few moments, I placed a few bills in his palm and bid him farewell.

I visited my former colleague in her downtown apartment. She recounted reports of uranium-tipped bullets burrowed within the rubble along the main boulevard. The hair on my arms bristled as I remembered the T-shirt that my father had worn in the early seventies. Across the front of the T-shirt, block letters had read: LONG RODS DO IT BETTER.

My father had been a set-up man at a munitions plant in Minneapolis. For years, he wore a sensor taped inside the interior of his wedding band. The sensor was removed and tested for exposure to uranium on a monthly basis.

More than a quarter of a century later, I contemplated the possibility that my father had had a hand in the manufacture of the Long Rods that lay fallow in the rubble along the streets of Belgrade. Their uranium tips, forever gleaming, in the heart of the city that I had been forced to flee.

BLIND RETURN

East crossing West at two rivers a crux
Rubble on curbsides torn windows and walls
Bleeding of hearts blind return left in flux—
From gleaming tips—*Long Rod Bullets*—life falls.
Turning back time with the skin of bare hands
Life is worth living although it is lost
Headstones on hillsides on still, fertile lands
Fruit of late harvests at double the cost.
Vapid, the sidewalks, death treading cement
Sky-colored canopies float on thin air
Pebbles on footsteps, a waltz of lament
Fingers stir foam in cracked cups as I stare.
Brandy in goblets, grilled kilos of meat,
Dried plums distilled from my tears bittersweet.

Belgrade, Serbia (Former Yugoslavia), 2001

BULGARIA

0	100 km
0	60 miles

ROMANIA

SERBIA

MACEDONIA

GREECE

TURKEY

BLACK SEA

To Odesa (Ukraine)

To Istanbul

BUCHAREST

SOFIA

Constanta

Ferry

Danube River

Stara Planina

Pirin Mountains

Rila Mountains

Rodopi Mountains

Sredna Gora

Valley of Roses

Mt Botev (2376m)
Mt Bogdan (1603m)
Mt Musala (2925m)
Mt Vihren (2914m)
Mt Vitosha (2290m)
Mt Kom (2015m)

Chapter Seven

BEYOND THE BLACK SEA

Sofia 1999–2001

My future uncertain, a month after I was evacuated from Belgrade for the third time, I accepted an assignment in a neighboring country to cover as the interim country director. I was slated to be stationed in Sofia for two months. My new-found friends assured me that I would be among them for two years—predictions that in time would ring true.

The large bright flowers on the sundress encased Kathryn's small frame. Her husband, Bob, stood beside her in the garden, slightly bearded and extremely fit from his marathon training. These were the first two people that I met in Belgrade. I had been invited to a private club to celebrate the Fourth of July holiday. The following week, I became a member. The following year, I was voted onto the board.

I also supported the youth orchestra as a member of the board. The conductor had been born and raised in Bulgaria, but he primarily lived in the US, where he was also the conductor of a youth symphony in Chicago. When I met him, he captured my heart. We became friends. I went to see him backstage with a single rose the first time that I attended a performance that he conducted in Sofia. After concerts it was difficult, however, to talk with him alone—he remained surrounded with professional friends and well-wishers for hours.

Unlike mine, his life was scheduled three years in advance. When he wasn't attending special dinners or evening events, we met for brief chats. When we were able to speak to each other on the phone, it was often well after midnight. We once took a walk to a favored place from his childhood. Our visit to the secluded area in the middle of a central park in Sofia, where one could find a bevy of miniature wooden houses, had left him disappointed. The mystical village had not weathered the years well.

He told me about his recent bid in the US to become the conductor of the Philadelphia Philharmonic. He outlined his strategy and discussed the music he had chosen to conduct in the audition. I understood nothing of the technical aspects of his work. I only knew that he was passionate and bold.

He once told me that he could not survive if he were not able to return to his native Bulgaria on a regular basis. Based on my yearning for home, I understood his desire to be in two places at one time. We met again, but my love for travel was not to converge with his love for music.

As an investor, profiting from tech stocks like many others at the time, I was invited to join a group of men who met weekly to discuss investing since I was reeling in as much as, or more in gains than, any of them. My intuition and capacity for risk allowed me to successfully take positions on start-up companies.

My job was manageable with a full and competent national staff. I was not required to work long hours. After the office closed, I had nothing but time. I began researching stocks in the evenings, building my portfolio late into the night. I bought and sold stocks online, rolling proceeds that often hit double digits into new positions.

As the summer unfolded, my portfolio grew. Stocks such as Juniper, Intel, and Ciena continued to post gains beyond any reasonable business model. I speculated on biotech stocks. I invested in Wells Fargo and Target Stores—two Minnesota-based companies that I knew from home.

I watched the ticker go up and down on a technology company that was developing Internet telephony. When the price fell under a dollar, I gobbled it up—believing that one day the technology would become a reality. The stock started to move, first doubling then tripling my portfolio. When the stock price reached $50 a share, I was sitting on a $50,000 gain. I talked to one of the more experienced businessmen whom I had met at the club.

"How do you know when to sell a stock?" I asked.

"Sometimes you just have to follow your gut," he said.

I had been watching the technology stocks continue to climb for months. I was not a seasoned or well-educated investor, but I sensed that there was not a sufficient foundation behind the high gains. More importantly, I learned an important lesson about myself—I didn't want to be rich. All I needed was to secure my financial future.

It was 1999. The end of the year was approaching with fears that the year 2000—Y2K—would usher in mammoth disruptions in our increasingly wired world. Companies clamored to invest in both hardware and software to cushion the blow of the mayhem anticipated when the clock struck midnight on December 31.

Before the end of the year, I sold off half of my Internet telephony stock at $50 a share. In January, I dumped the remaining half of the shares. A week later, the stock fell to $2 a share. As the larger technology bubble burst, the lucrative gains that my fellow investors and I had enjoyed over the past year dissipated.

One of the more conservative members of the group had begun to move his assets into cash. No one else in the group had followed his lead. Within days, my portfolio deflated. But as others experienced immediate and massive losses, following the sale of the Internet telephony stock, my slide to the world of bricks-and-mortar investing was a bit smoother—if only on paper.

On Sundays, I met Bob and Kathryn at the club for brunch. As the day progressed, we amassed a large group of friends. When the club closed, we gathered at someone's home, drinking and socializing late into the night. We had progressive dinners and traveled to Greece for long weekends, gliding over the border in the vehicles of our embassy friends.

I met Jason. We drank premium grape brandy by the bottle in lieu of wine over dinner. We went to the opera and the symphony on a weekly basis. I met Harry and Frankie. We gathered in groups of up to ten and flew off to Prague and Istanbul, where we explored the city, sampled the local cuisine, and drank large mugs of cold beer over long weekends.

Frankie and I were inseparable. An unlikely pair, while I had lived and worked in a number of countries overseas, he found it hard to understand how people could be expatriates. He loved his home in Wexford with its ample garden and large compost pit. An environmentalist, he had accepted a one-year assignment in Bulgaria with the Irish government. But, unlike me, he counted the days until he could return to his home and his extensive network of longtime friends.

One night when I was sitting with Frankie at a party, I told him that it was time for me to leave Bulgaria. It had been two years since my arrival, and I was ready for something new. Frankie agreed. For months he had been encouraging me to go home.

Frankie reached for the bottle of pear brandy on the bar in front of us. After filling my crystal goblet, he topped off his own. He placed his fingers around the short stem of his glass and sat for a moment, staring at the clear liquid. Then, he picked it up, emptied it, and placed it back down on the bar in front of him. He turned and looked over at me, eyes sparkling.

Frankie's assignment would be completed in the late fall. He only had one more scheduled trip back to Wexford before he returned home indefinitely. Over the summer, his home would remain empty, his garden unattended. He refilled our glasses. It was settled. Ireland would be a tranquil respite from my hectic overseas life.

We arranged to return to Wexford together. I packed my belongings and sent my personal effects back to a storage facility in Washington, DC. When I could not return to Belgrade, my colleagues had packed up my things and sent them to the same storage facility. From Sofia, I was consolidating yet another period of my life with the things that I had left behind.

At the airport, I sat down to await the flight. As I slid into my seat, my back was filled with pulsating pain. The stress of living and working in Belgrade had settled deeply into my muscles. And although I enjoyed my time in Sofia, I was never certain of the time that I would continue to stay. As I began to relax, the stress born out of insecurity and uncertainty morphed into shooting pains that ran up and down the sinews of my back.

In Wexford, we dropped our bags at the house and drove to the nearby market for provisions. In the parking lot, Frankie looked at me over the roof of the car. "It's so strange to be here with you," he said. "When we were in Bulgaria, I couldn't wait for you to go to Wexford, but now that you are here, it somehow seems odd."

I understood that he needed to spend time alone, reconnecting with his life in Wexford without me. I also needed to be alone—to think. I spent long hours in the mornings exploring sunny Wexford, a delightfully accessible walking town situated on the sea. My friend Kitty arrived from Washington, DC. We rented a car and traveled throughout the south of the country, returning to Wexford in time to see Frankie off.

After Kitty returned to the US and Frankie returned to Bulgaria, I was left in Ireland alone. Stumbling at a crossroads, I was living in Frankie's house and driving Frankie's car when all he wanted was to be back in the place where I was living aimlessly. At the end of the summer, I, too, left Wexford. Having nowhere else to go, I went home.

NOTES ON

Silent Music

Denitsa Angelkova is a brilliant pianist. If pressed, she would grace me and other colleagues with impromptu recitals at dinner parties when we were out. These were some of my most memorable moments in Bulgaria. My birthday was one such occasion. As was custom, I organized a dinner for close friends and colleagues where we drank pear brandy and ate *shopska* salad—a rendition of fresh cucumbers and tomatoes doused with vinegar and crumbled with feta cheese.

To capture our shared passion for music, I wrote this sonnet for Deni. I based it on my favorite quote by Miles Davis, who had said, "Don't play what's there, play what's not there."

Years earlier, Andy Frankel had taught me the timing of jazz. We were driving to a concert where Miles Davis was headlining. Andy kept time to the music wafting from the jazz tape he had popped into the dashboard of the car, counting the beats in dozens rather than the typical eight beats in other forms of popular music.

As he drove, Andy's finger pressed the air with each pulse. He raised his hand higher on the first beat of each new measure as he illustrated, with complete certainty, the technical basis of the form.

As we entered the outdoor arena, a cool breeze settled on a light wind. A trio took the stage. As the music flowed out into the night, the audience waved their fingers in unison as I waited for *Kind of Blue* or remnants of *Sketches of Spain.*

Miles Davis took the stage to a great deal of applause. It went unacknowledged. Rather, he raised his horn, turned his back, and began to play.

As he strolled across the stage, propelling disparate notes into the night air, I could only make out a glimmer of his silhouette as he teetered with his horn on the edge of darkness. Sitting back, I searched for the structure in the sound, but I also listened to the silence.

"Silent Music" attempts to capture the quiet between, within, and after each beat.

SILENT MUSIC

Imagine a kiss being blown—
Words gone missing between the lines
The backside is all that is shown
As notes shed the skin of confines.
Leave me in peace to plod along
Beside the music of choices
Propelled by a burst void of song—
Space welcomes notable voices.
Closeness is but approximate
The silence is felt in my heart,
The sound of a lone predicate
Defines the vastness of my art.
Deaf, to the sunlight, still I stare
At that which is, and is not there.

Sofia, Bulgaria, 1999

FORCES OF NATURE

Forces of nature, winds of change
Kindness gone awry is bitter.
Protracted wings are no less strange
Tumbleweeds that bounce and skitter.
A dried ink well, a quill so thin—
Tall and cool a glass of water
Parchment crackles against burnt skin,
Ashen tears refill the blotter.
Exploding thunder, angry stares,
Muffled voices that resonate.
Wooden birds released in thin air
Fall from grace with a thud of late.
Forces of nature know not bounds
As angels spar in match point rounds.

Sofia, Bulgaria, 2000

CHRIST-AGE PRAGUE SPRING

The striking clock calls out your time is near
Apostles pass as death rings out the bell
Christ-age Prague spring cloaks cobblestones in fear
Stark monuments share stories none shall tell.
To enter heaven upon golden wings
Pass under archways laden with God's stone
A child's cry deafens ears of lesser kings—
Closed lids, blank armor decorates the throne.
Crossbow in hand, we aim with knobby knees
We plead with Kafka eyes below the sill
Infant of Prague, please separate the seas,
Hold up thy head, avert the rains by will.
Atop the Charles Bridge raindrops chill the air
As Russian boots storm through the open square.

Sofia, Bulgaria, 2001

KNIGHT'S CROSSING

Knight's crossing to rook over land
Advancing the heart thus retreats,
A ship of fools buried in sand—
Blood waxing, the rose of defeat.
Casting her net, dropping her ores,
She readies herself to come in
Writ by the moon, tall tales of yore
Depict rabble-rousing and sin.
Viking crusades glide the king's fleet
Through ice storms, a threat to the throne
Castaway pawns—Ireland to Crete—
Lay past lives to rest under stone.
Shield-less the knight lays down the law
As queens calmly cross for a draw.

Sofia, Bulgaria, 2001

Chapter Eight

FINDING MY WAY

Minneapolis 2001

I returned to Minneapolis in early September. When I wasn't working, I played tennis and practiced yoga. I bought a piano—a baby Yamaha—that fit perfectly in the far corner of my downtown apartment overlooking the Basilica of St. Mary. I found a piano teacher at the MacPhaile Center for Music who allowed me to schedule lessons around my international consulting schedule. And…I entered the world of Internet dating.

Projected in its entirety, my short Internet dating life can be summed up as follows: the Photographer; the Gumshoe; the Banker; the Snowboard Salesman; the Electrician; Jake, the Optician; and Ski Mask. When I had initially posted my profile, I noted my interests and outlined my international travels. For weeks, I did not get any hits, so I changed my strategy, erasing my accomplishments and international work references. Instead, I stated: *I love to travel, and someday I hope to visit Europe.*

The change yielded incredible results—a dozen men responded in the following days to tell me how much they each felt that we had in common. Following my date with Ski Mask, I opted out of the service.

I had enjoyed the dates—I love meeting new people, but it was difficult for me to relate to the men who had sought me out. Although most of them had asked about my international background, none had posed a second question after asking: "What was it like?" None of them spoke any language other than English, except for one man, Ski Mask, who had traveled to Mexico for a week, where he had used his high-school Spanish.

I had been intrigued with a number of profiles, and although I may have been able to flatter a man, the flattery did not translate into a date. I was only able to arrange dates with men who had initially contacted me.

My date with the Photographer was at a local bar. I entered the bar looking for a six-foot-one-inch man with blond hair. I was met by a man who was much thinner and not much taller than me. By chance, the sister of a close friend who I hadn't seen in a number of years was at the bar. After hugging her excitedly in greeting, as I swept my arm around to present my date, I nearly smacked him in the head. During our second date, I maneuvered myself close to a mirror. I called out to my new friend to stand next to me. Looking into the mirror, I placed him at five foot nine inches.

The next day, I called my father.

"Pop," I said, "I've been dating a guy that I met on the Internet. His profile said that he was six foot one, but he is not much taller than me."

"Men always lie about their height," he said.

I was not sure what my father thought of my Internet dating exploits. Many of my friends and schoolmates had married young. But I had wanted to follow a different path, believing that one day I would saddle up next to someone who was going in the same direction that I was. When this didn't happen, I spoke to my father. I was in my late thirties when I asked him for advice.

"Pop, do you think that I will ever get married?" I asked.

He countered my question with one of his own. "How long are you going to wait for your knight in shining armor to appear?"

"I don't know. How long do you think I should wait?"

"It's a myth," he said. "You can stop waiting. It's not going to happen."

"Well," I said, "thanks a lot for telling me now!"

I continued to troll the dating website. My next date was with the Gumshoe. He worked in a well-to-do part of town. After we had settled in at the bar, he ordered me a drink without asking me what I wanted. I let it slide. In the tagline of my profile, I had noted: *Champagne? Sure!* I downed the effervescent liquid from the glass that had been placed in front of me on the bar. My date ordered me another. Before I could speak, he looked over at me.

"You're not used to being with someone who takes control, are you?"

The man looked like Bill Clinton. The former president, however, had much more charisma.

"No," I said, raising the second glass of champagne to my lips. I took a long sip before looking back over at him. "I am not."

Throughout the evening my date spoke of three things: his ex-wife, his money, and how she wasn't going to get any part of it. The next day, he invited me to travel with him to an island somewhere in the Bahamas. I told him that I was between jobs and could not afford the cost. The following day he asked me again. For a second time, I politely refused.

The Banker was never available between the hours of five o'clock in the evening on Friday and nine o'clock in the morning on Monday. I imagined him to be on furlough during the week. The Snowboard Salesman must have misread my profile—he was looking for someone much younger. I carried on a correspondence with the Electrician for weeks, but he did not suggest that we meet. When he became more serious with a woman he was dating who was more closely aligned with his religious beliefs, he broke off the banter.

By the time Jake asked me out, I was exasperated. Jake was an attractive man, not much taller than me, but this had been clearly stated in his profile. He was also a runner. He wanted to meet, but I was not convinced that we would be a good match. I asked him to list two of his favorite places in Minneapolis. The Mall of America was at the top of his list, and he liked to go to the community rose garden next to Lake Harriet in the middle of the city. Although I wasn't a shopper, I was a hopeless romantic. I agreed to meet him in person.

Jake and I dated for a number of weeks. One evening, while we were talking on the phone, Jake recounted a traumatic experience that he had had the year before. While he was driving home from work one evening, a boy had run out onto the highway in front of his vehicle. He had swerved and missed him, but another boy had been running behind the first boy across the highway, and Jake had hit him.

Later that night, Jake went to the hospital. When Jake told the police officer that he thought that he had killed the boy, the police officer assured him that the boy was alive. The police officer brought him to the room where the boy was receiving treatment, but Jake had not believed that he was the boy he had hit. When he recounted the story to me a year later, Jake still believed that the police officer had lied to him.

"Jake," I said. "The boy is still alive. If the police officer lied to you, it would not only be unconscionable, it would be immoral."

There was silence on the other end of the line.

"Tell me the name of the boy that you hit," I said. "I will go with you to find his grave to prove that he is not dead. I will help you find him. You can arrange to meet with him and his parents to apologize if you want. Jake, you did not kill the boy that you hit."

The next day, Jake called to break up with me.

"Jake," I said. "You can't tell me what you told me yesterday and then break up with me."

I understood his trauma, and I had wanted to help him. Perhaps I already had. A week earlier, I had invited Jake over for dinner. He had arrived with flowers. After dinner, Jake sat on the couch, looking out into the sky, marveling at the planes that flew past my apartment building at seemingly eye level in the distance. While he was relaxed, I was uptight. Something had triggered a memory from Rwanda earlier that day. I sat down next to Jake on the couch. As he reached over to put his arm around me, I began to cry. When I was able to speak, he listened quietly as I told him about the day that I had visited the women in prison.

A week later, he had done the same with me. It was the first time that he had recounted the story of the accident to anyone. We never went in search of the grave or to try to find the boy together, but after a few weeks, he called me again. We saw each other a few more times, but we were not well matched for the long term. So he amicably went his own way, and I went mine.

When I met Ski Mask, I shook hands with a man of medium height and medium build, sporting a short-sleeved sweatshirt and a pair of thick glasses. I had needed to wait until he spotted me in the bar. In his profile, he had only posted one photo. Taken on a snowy mountaintop, the ski mask that he wore in the photo completely covered his face.

I had told Ski Mask that I could only meet him briefly, since I had recently returned from overseas and was jetlagged. He assured me that he understood, having traveled to Europe a few times himself. We sat at the bar, struggling to find a shared topic of interest. Unsuccessful in identifying something new to talk about, we continued our earlier discussion about jet-lag. A half hour later, I told him that mine had kicked in, and I needed to go home. When the check came, he divided it in half—less a tip—and asked me for my exact share. I handed him a ten-dollar bill and without waiting for change, said good-bye and left.

To reenter the professional world stateside, I began informational interviewing, marking time with cover letters, updated resumes, and cold calls. I arranged meetings with professionals in the fields I wanted to break into.

A friend provided me with a contact at the Science Museum of Minnesota. A few days after I returned home, I phoned him. He agreed to meet. I spoke about my experiences in international development and asked for advice on how I might redirect my professional life in the US. "You need to meet Leslie," he said. "I will send you her contact." He stood up, shook my hand, and wished me luck.

Leslie was the director of development, a fundraiser—an entirely different ilk from skills in development overseas—but my list of contacts had been exhausted after my first meeting, so I called her.

"Hello, this is Leslie. Today is Monday, September 10th, and I am in the office today. Please leave a message and I will get back to you as soon as possible."

I hung up, preferring to catch her on voice for our first conversation. I tried the next day.

"Hello, this is Leslie. Today is Tuesday, September 11th, and I am in the office today. Please leave a message and I will get back to you as soon as possible."

As soon as I hung up, the phone rang.

"Turn on the television," my sister said. "I'm coming home."

I crossed the room and turned on the television. Smoke was wafting across the screen. I sat on the edge of the couch, trying to make sense of what I was seeing. One of the Twin Towers in the financial district in New York City was burning. I heard the door slam. My sister came down the stairs into the den, her gun belt wrapped tightly around her hips.

"A plane crashed into one of the Twin Towers," she said. As she sat down next to me, I rose. Hands clasped around my face, I stood in horror as the second tower was hit—flames, smoke, chaos—the first tower continued to burn.

It went down.

"No!" I gasped. Flames flew out of the second tower. "No—No!—NO!"

As I stood watching, the second tower began its slide. After the second tower had reached the ground, I lowered myself onto the couch.

For days afterward, I stayed up with Peter Jennings, following the story late into the night. If he took a break, I took a break, sleeping for a few hours before getting up and returning to the coverage. As I watched from the sofa in my sister's den in rural Minnesota, from his chair at ABC News in New York City, Peter Jennings anchored a nation.

For three days, the only transmission on network television was the coverage of the story of the Twin Towers. The next day, *The Minneapolis Star-Tribune* ran a harrowing full-page spread of dazed New Yorkers running wildly through the streets—screaming, covered in ash. My e-mail in-box filled with messages from around the world.

My friends from Ireland called. I had only been home for a week. "I'm so sorry!" they each told me.

The day that the stock market reopened, I bought stock in Heinz, even though I was sure to lose money on the investment.

I grasped for ideas to show support to New Yorkers and others affected by the attacks, wanting desperately to erase what was happening.

On Friday evening at six, regular programming resumed on network television as my life as a global nomad, alongside thousands of New Yorkers and millions of Americans, continued its steady transformation. Airport regulations and procedures would change, and each time that I traveled internationally from that day forward, as I passed through security, I would be reminded of that terrible day.

The following Monday, I called Leslie. Her voice-mail clicked on after three rings. I left a message. Minutes later, she returned my call.

"Hi, this is Leslie," she said.

"Hi Leslie, thanks so much for getting back to me." I told her a little about my experiences in Africa and asked if she would have time to meet with me as I continued to explore a career change in Minneapolis. We arranged to meet later that week in the lobby of the museum. The morning of our meeting, I received a phone call.

"Julie, this is Leslie. I'm sorry, but I can't meet today," she said. Her voice trailed off. I heard her speaking in the distance to a security guard. Her voice became strong again. "I will call you when I can."

She hung up.

Leslie called me the next day to explain. A jelly-like substance had been spotted in the lobby of the museum, near the garbage area of the museum café. Earlier that day, a man of Middle Eastern descent had been followed on the security camera as he walked through the museum lobby with a briefcase.

Without stopping to buy a ticket to enter the special exhibit, he placed a briefcase on the floor next to the Turkish artifacts included in the exhibit and left the building.

The security team called in the bomb squad. Breathing through an oxygen supply inside of their suits, the hazardous waste team opened the briefcase. It contained a dirty coffee cup and some documents in Arabic—a manual of sorts for a non-nefarious purpose. The jelly-like substance was tested. It was jelly. The museum reopened the next day.

Later that week, after parking in the museum garage ramp, I slid through the glass doors and up the elevator to the main level of the museum. Reaching the small café in the lobby, I ordered a coffee and sat down to wait. As I watched from a small table, a young woman passed under the archway of a side stairway. Gliding through the crowds, she crossed the wide lobby with authority. As she approached the lobby café in her tailored suit, I stood up in black jeans and a black jacket. I held out my hand.

"Leslie?"

"Hi," she said. "It's nice to meet you."

She shook my hand firmly.

"Tell me more about Africa," she said. "I've always wanted to go there."

She was interested in Rwanda. I told her it was difficult to discuss, being that the memories of the genocide were still so fresh in my mind, even though it had been many years since I had left the country. I had tried to temper my stories over the years, but I was not able to moderate myself if I had a willful listener. There was too much to say and few who could stand to listen.

"I have a little time," she said. "Tell me what you can."

Leslie stretched out our meeting.

"I want your life," she said.

I looked back at her.

"Are you kidding?" I replied. "I want yours!"

And for a moment, I think that we both actually thought it possible. It was the stuff of movies. A screenplay that could be written but would never be produced. How many times had I looked at the life of another woman, wishing instead that it were me who had been cast in the role that another had so successfully landed?

A few months later, my sister called.

"I might have to go to Washington, DC," she said.

"Why?" I asked.

"The twentieth hijacker was in our jail. I monitored his calls."

He was Moroccan. My sister worked at the county jail, which was also a federal holding facility where illegal immigrants were detained pending trial or deportation.

"I might need to testify in front of the grand jury," she added.

"Great," I said flatly. "That is just great—I don't want you to go."

She told me that she would not have a choice if called to testify.

"Fine," I told her. "If you're called, then I'll go with you."

I told her that I would sit next to her in the courtroom and if the potential hijacker looked our way, I would put my index finger under my right eye and pull it down my face. I said that I would whisper, *"Hashuma, alik!"* shame on you in Moroccan Arabic.

"It'll do nothing to keep you safe, but it'll give him pause," I said. "It's something that his mother would have said to him in Morocco when he was young, after he had done something bad. It'll freak him out."

It wasn't the first time that my sister had met someone from one of the countries where I had lived and worked. A year earlier, a male Rwandan was being held in the jail on an immigration issue when he was indicted on charges of genocide by the International Criminal Court.

"I told him that my sister used to work in Rwanda," she said one night as we were chatting on the phone. "We used to talk a lot, we would joke," she explained. "He was a nice gentleman, but he kept to himself, especially after I told him that I knew what had happened during the genocide in Rwanda."

When I returned home in the evenings, the lights of the Basilica shone brightly into my apartment. The view was magnificent, but to my eyes it only reflected pain. Thousands of people had been massacred in Catholic churches in Rwanda. The implications tore at my core. I thought of Assumpta, her name alone a testament to the deeply religious traditions in Rwanda.

One morning, as I was sitting at home the sun streamed into my apartment, tickling the dome of the Basilica before landing on the carpet next to me. Crawling on my knees toward the phone book that lay on the floor in front of me, I pulled it onto my lap and flipped to the back section in search of service providers. I pulled my finger over the pages from top to bottom until I found the listing that I sought: *Post Traumatic Stress*.

Jim Moore had worked with Vietnam Veterans and was a specialist in neurolinguistic programming, a discipline that I had explored while working as a Peace Corps trainer in Morocco. As I recounted the death of my close colleague, Assumpta, I felt comforted. Jim understood my grief, even though it had been years since the incident.

I was instructed to do three things to work through my grief. First, gather trinkets or other items that reminded me of Assumpta and find a quiet place to sit. Second, tell Assumpta all of the things that I had wanted to say to her before she had died. Third, say my good-byes. I thanked Jim and left his office, grateful for a way forward. It would be weeks, however, before I would be ready to face the task.

It was late morning when the time for leave-taking arrived. The large windows of my apartment were open. As a fresh breeze filtered throughout the living room, I went into my closet and rummaged through a small box of trinkets that I had brought back from Rwanda. I pulled out a plastic keychain stamped with the word "Uganda." Assumpta had died in Uganda. I pulled out a prayer card with the Virgin Mary—a Christmas greeting from a staff member in Rwanda. I set the prayer card next to the keychain on the coffee table in front of me.

"Assumpta," I said aloud, "before I begin, is there anything that you would like to say to *me?*"

Without a breath, the bells of the Basilica began to ring.

I submitted my resume to a temporary agency in search of short-term work. A week later, I stopped into the office to ask if there were any jobs for me. The young receptionist pulled me aside.

"I wanted to tell you that you have a typo on your resume," she said, pointing at *Tbilisi*, the capital city noted on my resume in front of the country of Georgia. "You might want to correct that," she suggested. "There is no *Tbilisi* in Georgia."

I smiled as she handed me the paper.

"Thanks," I said. "I'll take care of it."

I reached out to my international contacts to return overseas as an international consultant. I was hired on a number of short-term contracts, but I was not able to fully support myself financially. I covered my monthly expenses by selling off my investments. The following spring, when my investment portfolio was depleted, I called my mother for advice.

I had found a listing for a job in a remote area of Central Africa. For years, I had yearned to return to a French-speaking country. The five years that I had spent in Eastern Europe had not allowed me to keep up my French. I wanted to live and work in French again, so that I would not further erode my language skills.

"Honey, of course you need to go back overseas," my mother said. "It's where you've always been happiest."

For the first time in my international career, I was relieved.

"As hard as it'll be for me to see you leave again," she added, "I've always known that this is who you are."

Within weeks, I packed up my apartment, put my personal belongings in storage, and departed for the Republic of Congo.

NOTES ON

Silent Echo

Echo Bodine, a local psychic and ghost buster, was speaking at a symposium in Minneapolis. In her lecture, she recounted the story of how she came to realize that she was a psychic. She also talked of her spirit guides. She said that these spirits provided her with messages to guide her in her work. She told the audience their names.

At once, I understood the connection that I had felt with her upon entering the auditorium. Teddy and Lilly, the names of Echo's spirit guides, are also the names of my father's parents.

A year later, I attended a second lecture with my sister, Susan. We met up with Echo in the corridor during the break.

"We hate to bother you," I said, "but my sister and I wanted you to know that the names of our grandparents are Ted and Lilly."

"No bother at all," Echo said as she bristled by my sister and me. Stopping suddenly, Echo turned and folded her arms tightly against her chest. "I just got goose bumps," she said.

SILENT ECHO

Blinding light, blinking, cool vapor, a swirl
Hidden in consciousness, dark matter, chants
Whispering voices as pages unfurl
Parchment—lost music, the echo of dance.
See me not, yet I dry tears from heaven
Symphonic memories, time passes by
Garden of Eden, death of a maiden
Shrill sounding trumpets have muffled my cries.
If this I ask, will you tell me your name?
Anchor my heart, hang my soul within reach
Tether my thoughts, I consent to bear blame.
Where lie the lessons that you bring to teach?
A reed on the wind that floats out of sight,
Bid thee farewell in the deep of the night.

Minneapolis, Minnesota, 2001

NOTES ON

The Likes of Me

One of my favorite novels, *A Suitable Boy* by Vikram Seth, chronicles three generations of an Indian family. Seth, a venerable poet, is no stranger to iambic pentameter, weaving a number of poems into the novel and writing the contents section in rhyme. While living in San Francisco, he also wrote *The Golden Gate,* a novel entirely in sonnets.

While reading *A Suitable Boy,* I lived in Washington, DC. Most often preferring to meet friends after work for drinks, instead I rushed home each night for weeks to read. Seth's characters became my friends. I grew up with them, got married with them, struggled with them, and died with them.

The trilogy by Nobel Prize for Literature winner Naguib Mafouz, *Palace Walk, Palace of Desire,* and *Sugar Street* is no less enticing. These volumes, which begin sometime after the turn of the century, chronicle three generations of an Egyptian family as the country struggles for independence. And, like *A Suitable Boy,* the trilogy weaves history, politics, culture, and tradition into a literary labyrinth.

The reference included in the third quatrain of the sonnet is at the close of chapter seventy in *Palace Walk.* Famay Ahmed, son of Al-Sayyid Ahmed, a businessman and main character in the trilogy, is protesting in the streets of Cairo. As the crowd swells, police arrive and begin firing on the protesters. Famay watches as his brothers in opposition stumble and disperse in panic. His resolve remains, his passion and commitment unflappable. He stands tall as he sees his life pass in front of his eyes. The reader travels with him inside of his conscience as he floats in time, reminiscing until the reader realizes that he himself has fallen onto the ground alongside the fallen son—and only one of them is still breathing.

The Spirit Catches You and You Fall Down, an anthropological account by novelist Anne Fadiman, relates the cross-cultural experiences of the immigrant family of a young Hmong girl as they navigate across cultures from their new home in California. Aspects of their cultural clashes with American society are recounted through their experiences with the US health care system. As an epileptic prone to particularly aggressive seizures, the child is revered in her own culture as a shaman. Yet, her parents are not able to ensure that the traditions of their culture are respected and preserved when seeking medical attention for their child.

At every turn, the family is faced with misunderstanding, the situation, no doubt, further complicated by a lack of understanding by Americans—including myself until I learned differently—who believe the Hmong to be Vietnamese, a people with an entirely different language and traditions.

The story straddles the war in Southeast Asia and present day as it brings to light the struggle of the Hmong people. In one segment, the story of a Hmong family crossing the Mekong River as they flee their homeland is told. A husband and father talks of how he tragically loses his wife and children while crossing the river. The broken man recalls how he had often told his wife how much he loved her more than life itself. While crossing the river, he is not able to pull his wife on his back, and he is faced with the decision of saving his own life over hers. Mired in guilt, the grieving man later laments, "I guess it wasn't true."

I was stunned by the honesty of the man's recollection. And I thought, we may choose to believe the best for ourselves and we may easily pronounce how we would react in such an extreme predicament. But it is only when we are faced with a choice such as this that we can ever truly know what we would do.

THE LIKES OF ME

To ancient cultures I held out my hand.
Walled cities, desert, the ocean, the sea,
Beyond every mountain the promised land
Has welcomed with wonder the likes of me.
Cracked leather, charred heels, a hole in my boot,
Retracing my steps I cannot find home,
In richness of soil where I take root
The world writ large I continue to roam.
Taking my leave as the crowd stumbles by,
I offer alms at the foot of the throne
A suitable boy, a latticework sky—
Will I love you more than life, save my own?
Beyond every mountain, waves from the sea,
Have welcomed with wonder the likes of me.

Minneapolis, Minnesota, 2002

THE PIANO STUDENT

Mozart's life work was built upon a tone
Among his many tools a harpsichord
Debussy, Bach, Rameau, a metronome
Stacked on a root in thirds—a major chord.
A dotted note and eighth complete a whole
Half common time, relax and read with ease
A healing breath is tonic for the soul
As gingerly my fingers tap the keys.
An offering of gifts within each score
A song, a dance, a story to be told
A measured phrase first calm ends in a roar
When weighted to my limbs, three *fff*s hang bold.
The greatest joy stems from each inner duel,
A world content on my piano stool.

Minneapolis, Minnesota, 2003

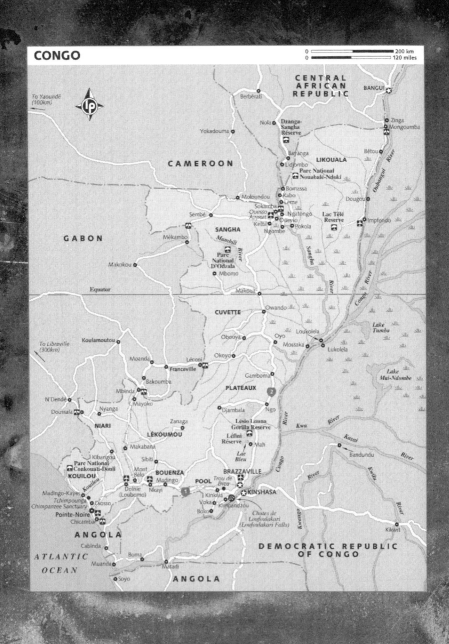

Chapter Nine

AFTER THE EMERGENCY RESPONSE

Brazzaville 2003–05

Once I was back overseas, I continued my piano studies. On Saturdays, I went for a run or played tennis at the five-star hotel before going into the bar, where the waiters allowed me to practice on the grand piano that sat idly in the corner of the room. I found a teacher—a Ukrainian woman who had met and married a Congolese man in the Soviet Union thirty years earlier.

With little hope of finding a piano tuner once I arrived in Brazzaville, I did not ship my piano into the densely humid climate of the Republic of Congo. Instead, I worked with my teacher on an electric piano I had imported from Europe. Upon my departure two years later, the electric piano, repaired by rudimentary means after numerous abrupt power outages, was bequeathed to my teacher. She had had two pianos of her own, but both had been pillaged during the war.

It had been over two years since there had been open conflict in the streets of Brazzaville. Communities two hours outside of the capital in the remote Pool region, however, continued to experience on-going insecurity. Flare-ups between government and opposition forces occasionally spilled back into the capital. During these times, panic was instilled into the larger population as they relived the trauma of the pillages that they had endured during the war.

It was early afternoon during the dry season when rumors circulated in our office that groups of people were running down the street with their mattresses on their backs. This was reportedly happening in a neighborhood outside of the center of the city where most of the national staff lived.

I called the staff together.

"Go home and secure your homes and your families," I instructed. "You can all leave early today to pick up your children from school."

As I spoke, the logistics coordinator distributed pre-paid phone cards that we held in the safe for emergencies. I instructed the team to keep in touch through the warden system we developed in our security training. We confirmed the list of emergency numbers. I told the staff that I would continue to monitor the situation with heads of other international organizations and the UN.

"Come back tomorrow if you think that the roads are safe to travel," I said.

The staff disbursed, buzzing in anticipation as they prepared to leave the office.

I only had been in Brazzaville for a short time. When I arrived, we were broke. Major funding for displaced populations inside of the Republic of Congo had dried up. In countries where I had worked with long-term development projects, I had had sufficient funding for multi-year projects. I was able to pay staff and conduct planned activities that were managed out of a fully operational office.

As I moved into the world of emergency response—often entering a country two or more years after the initial emergency—I took over management as country programs were facing funding gaps, site closures, and staff layoffs. In more than one instance, I inherited a graveyard of broken-down vehicles and office equipment yet to be disposed.

During the initial emergency phase, funding requests from international sources are more easily mobilized when people are working to save lives. As the media attention wanes, funding for essential humanitarian needs dissipates. Funding streams connecting long-term development activities to short-term humanitarian needs are rarely reconciled. As a result, affected communities are often left without external support—their unbroken spirits their only collateral.

I was working with my team to design programs to meet the needs of women and children affected by the conflict. Competition for limited funding was fierce. Under deadline, we were in the process of writing a number of grant proposals to submit to donors. I also had agreed to host a global training program. I was tired. But I didn't realize how tired I was until the day after the international trainer arrived from the home office, and I couldn't get out of bed.

I had been exhausted for weeks. My eyes hurt. When I walked from my office to the front room to talk with a colleague or deposit a document in another department, I needed to sit down to rest before I was able to return to my office, which was only twenty feet away.

When I could no longer bear the exhaustion, I called my mother. "Mom, my eyes ache and I'm so tired," I said. "I don't know what to do."

My mother told me to rest. I said that I would, hung up, and went back to work.

The next day I had a pounding headache. My joints ached. I tried to stand up but couldn't. I lay back down and reached for my cell phone. I called a colleague and told him I was not feeling well. He informed the staff not to bother me.

I lay in bed all day, moaning. I had not called anyone during the day, and no one had called or come to my house to check on me. At ten in the evening, when the pain became worse, I called my colleague.

"I need a doctor," I said.

An hour later, there was a knock on my door. I crawled out of bed, crossed the living room, and slid the glass door open. Two of my colleagues stepped through the mosquito netting. A Congolese man in a lab coat, stethoscope hanging around his neck, followed them into the house. A woman in a lab coat trailed into the house after the man.

The man in the lab coat asked me to take off my dress. I unbuttoned the top buttons, exposing my breasts. The man placed a stethoscope on the moist, sweaty skin over my breastbone. My colleagues turned their backs. Flipping off her shoes and stretching out her feet, the woman slouched into the chair she had sat in immediately upon entering the room.

"*C'est Palu,*" he said, using the colloquialism for *paludisme*—malaria. The man told me that I had had it for some time. I buttoned the top of my dress. The man took one of my colleagues aside. He could set me up with a quinine drip in my living room. The woman in the lab coat would stay the night, the cost—one hundred US dollars. My colleague translated the treatment plan into English.

"No," I whispered back at him, looking over his shoulder at the woman who sat slouching in the chair across the room. "I don't want her in my house," I said.

The woman had shown no interest in my case since she had entered the house, and I did not trust that she would take care of me. My colleague asked the man if there were any pills that I could take.

"You can buy her quinine tablets tomorrow," the man said in French.

My colleague paid the man a nominal fee and escorted the couple out of the house.

The next morning, my colleague arrived at my house with a blister pack of quinine tablets. I started the course of treatment. Two days later, when my condition had not improved, I called a friend to ask for a referral.

"Do you know a doctor in Brazzaville?" I asked. "I need someone with experience."

There was a French doctor who had lived in Brazzaville for over thirty years that some of the expatriates had seen. He ran a private clinic but only held office hours for two hours each morning.

I called my driver.

The French doctor prescribed the World Health Organization recommended Coartem, an artemisinin-based combination therapy. His fee for the office visit was less than the equivalent of ten US dollars. I was relived to be treated by a doctor who understood the disease. I had been told that some countries in Africa still sanctioned the prescription of chloroquine, a drug that had been resistant to malaria in many parts of Africa for years.

A few days later, I returned to see the French doctor. The drug he had prescribed had not changed my condition. He prescribed another artemisinin-based combination therapy that he used for more difficult cases of malaria. Quinine in liquid form is a therapy reserved for the most serious cases. Once in your blood stream, although it is extremely harsh, it is also extremely effective. It can be too quickly prescribed, however, leaving health professionals no other options if the quinine fails.

I regretted not taking the harsher treatment that first night. But I knew so little about the disease or treatment options at the time. Amoebas, parasites, worms—yes. But it was my first experience with malaria. I started to eat foods to fortify my blood. For the first time in my life, I bought and cooked liver, a regime that I would incorporate into my lifestyle for many months afterward.

I fell ill with malaria again after fifteen days, sought treatment, and fell ill again fifteen days later. The illness continued to come in cycles. The doctors referred to it as recrudescence. My friends and colleagues also contracted the disease. If a person was infected with the parasite, in addition to the exhaustion and other aches and pains, there was no sparkle in his or her eyes.

Because malaria attacks the liver, I was not able to drink alcohol for weeks. I craved a cold beer—one of the only things that can quench a thirst on hot, humid nights. A week after completing my treatment, I was sitting outdoors on my patio, drinking a beer. Within minutes, I felt the alcohol course through my veins, unable to be metabolized. I fell over on the wicker couch and slept.

The first time I contracted malaria, I was out of work for a week. Each time that I fell ill with the disease subsequently, I took the afternoon off if the blood test came back positive. I visited the office administrator at the Doctors Without Borders compound and requested a stock of malaria treatment packs for emergencies. I bought and carried a treatment pack in my luggage for more than ten years afterward. I self-medicated when I was out in the field if I fell ill and was not near an adequate medical facility.

I grew thin. I had been sick on and off for months. I was scheduled to travel to Nairobi for a regional conference, but I was too ill to travel. Nonetheless, I decided to take the trip. I wanted to be in Nairobi if my condition worsened, since this is where I would be sent if I were to be medically evacuated.

My flight to Nairobi originated from Kinshasa. My driver arranged for me to cross the Congo River by speedboat. I had taken the trip before. I knew people who loved living and working in bustling, crazy, corrupt, overcrowded Kinshasa. I despised Kinshasa. Brazzaville, a five-minute speedboat ride across the Congo River, was a sleepy little town where one could sit and have a leisurely drink along the river. On the other side of the rapids less than a mile away, there were no restaurants or bars where one could relax along the banks of the river.

On both sides of the river, street children hopped on boats and barges, assuming roles as caretakers of the wheelchair-bound. Uninvited, men claimed luggage out of the hands of passersby and carried it onto the boats as porters. It was impossible to step onto a boat without being jostled. Once in Brazzaville, the crowds in the port area quickly dispersed. This was not the case on the other side.

We used a protocol service to facilitate our transit through immigration. My US passport generated interest. The immigration official wanted to see me in person. I had been invited to his office before. The immigration official had asked me for money, but I only had tipped him in time.

Papa, my contact with the protocol service, escorted me into the office. I stood in front of the immigration official, staring blankly. He asked me a question. I ignored him.

"Do you want to give me a little something?" he asked in French. "So I can buy a little drink?"

My eyes dropped like boulders onto his face.

"To expedite the process," he added.

"I'm sick," I said in English.

He asked me another question. I didn't respond. He stamped my passport and told Papa to take me away.

Due to the international flight schedule, I arrived in Nairobi two days before the start of the conference. I checked into my hotel and went to bed without getting up until late in the afternoon the following day. Although I was still ill, I attended the conference. I asked my regional director for a few days of leave to rest afterwward. My leave was approved, allowing me to regain some of my strength before I departed.

Two weeks after arriving in Nairobi, I flew back over central Africa, returning home to Brazzaville. But it would not be long before I would contract malaria again. I slept with a mosquito net. When I was outdoors between the hours of dusk and dawn, I sprayed my arms and legs with a repellent containing a high concentration of DEET. I took 100 milligrams of doxycycline each morning even though it burned in my stomach after sliding down my throat. But although my skin was clear, my blood continually became infected with malaria parasites.

I called a doctor at the home office. He suggested that I also treat the guards. We had a large staff of guards that rotated regularly. It would be impossible to completely eradicate the disease. I struggled through long days when I was not feeling well. At times, it was difficult to raise my hands and place them on the keyboard of my computer.

I was not alone. I discussed the challenge of working in an environment where malaria was endemic with one of my colleagues. "Can you imagine how much more we could accomplish," she said, "if we weren't falling ill with this damned malaria so often?"

I agreed. I would rather be working to improve programs and operations than to be running off for blood tests in the middle of the day every time that I got a headache. There was always so much more to be done and we were often understaffed. When my colleagues fell ill, I urged them to get tested to rule out malaria, which could enter the brain and become fatal. For my part, I knew that if I did not take care of myself, I would not be able to continue to do the work that I loved. Still, I continued to fall ill.

Our staff compound was at the end of a dirt road that trailed off into a wooded area. A number of Rwandan immigrants who had fled the refugee camps in the Democratic Republic of Congo—walking west across the continent rather than going home—had settled in small enclaves in makeshift shacks at the end of the road.

Next to my house, to the left, was a brothel where Faith purportedly had stayed. Men entertained women over a meal or a cold beer across the road from the brothel at a small, outdoor café. The Doctors Without Borders compound, at the other end of the dirt road, sidled up to the other side of the brothel. Lieutenant Davie occupied the house across the street from Doctors Without Borders.

I was notified by the night guard that a young girl had arrived at the gates of the center for street children. The program coordinator who managed the street children program activities was on leave, so I walked over to the center to speak with the girl. After she had been told to leave the brothel the night before, she had found her way to the center. The night guard had allowed her to take refuge there. The next morning, she slipped out of the gate before dawn. The following night, she returned. When I arrived, she was sitting in an exterior room that we left unlocked in the evenings.

I sat down next to her, but she didn't speak. I moved across the room and sat in a chair. I asked her where she was from. She got up, walked over, and stood in front of me. I pulled her onto my lap. She laid her head on my shoulder and began to cry.

As her small legs dangled off to the side, the soles of her bare feet tapped the skin on my legs. It burned. I had felt the sensation many times before. Small children often ran up to me to shake my hand when I was on a site visit in their village. If they had been playing in the dirt and had not washed their hands, when they touched my skin it created a burning sensation.

When I had discussed the sensation that I had experienced with one of my staff nurses in the field, she had told me that there were many microbes in the dirt. If a person's skin—the first layer of defense in a person's immune system—is not used to coming into contact with the microbes, she had said, the skin reacted.

I set Faith down and went into the center in search of some paper and a marker. When I came back out, I sat with her to draw a picture. She was despondent. I placed the paper on the cement floor between us. I spelled out her name in block letters and filled in the open spaces inside of each letter.

Before I left, I gave her a clean sheet of paper and a marker, and I asked her to draw me a picture. The next day, when I returned to the center, she was gone. The guard handed me a picture that she had drawn. Depicted in the picture was a family, living happily in a village. On the top of the page, in block letters, she had written my name.

A month later, the program coordinator informed me that Faith was coming to the center to participate in the daily activities. Faith had told her that when I had held her on my lap, I had reminded her of her mother, who had died when Faith was very young.

Faith was placed in an orphanage in the area. During a follow-up visit to check on her progress, the program coordinator learned that Faith had had a fight with a boy at the orphanage. After she had hit the boy, she had run away.

It was a weekend, and the center was closed when the guard called me to tell me that Faith had returned. When I arrived at the center, she was playing with some sticks on the side of the building. I went over and sat down in the dirt next to her.

"Ca va?" Are you okay? I asked.

She looked up at me but did not speak. I told her that I knew that she had had a problem at the orphanage. She stared back at me. I asked her where she had been. No response. I asked her what she was going to do. She replied that she was going to live at the center.

"Honey, I'm sorry, but you can't stay here," I told her in French. "It is not safe for you here at night."

We had arranged for the guards to direct children to a center that had adequate accommodations for street children in the evenings. Our center only offered daily educational and psychosocial activities in addition to showers, a noon meal, and laundry facilities.

Faith became defiant. She told me that she hadn't liked the boy, and she didn't want to go back to the orphanage.

"Honey," I repeated in French, "I'm sorry, but you can't live here."

I called the director of the orphanage to tell him that Faith was with me at the center. I asked him if he would consider taking her back. He told me that she had fought with a number of children before she had hit the boy and run away. He was concerned that she would make trouble again if she returned. I asked him if he would allow her to return if she apologized to the boy she had struck.

He agreed.

We arranged for her to return to the orphanage later that afternoon. I hung up the phone and turned to Faith.

"Faith," I said, "the director misses you and wants you to go back to live at the orphanage."

I waited before continuing in French. "But there is a problem," I said. "Honey, you can't hit the other children. It's not nice, and I know that you are nicer than that."

She looked down at the dirt.

"If you go back, you need to apologize to the boy that you hit." I took a deep breath. "Will you go back?"

She pulled her finger through the dirt in front of her, looked up at me, and nodded her head once.

"Okay," I said in French. "I will be back to pick you up in the afternoon at four."

When I returned with the driver later that day, Faith was out in the backyard of the compound attending to her laundry. The sun reflected off of her dark skin as the few items of her clothing fluttered in the breeze. She looked so focused—it was hard to believe that she was only eight years old.

I had never considered adopting a child until I met Faith. Yet, Faith had come from a family in a neighboring village. She had a home, even though she had been sent away. Many of the street children that we worked with had been blamed for traumatic events visited upon their families. In the face of illness, death, or financial ruin, it was often a child who was blamed. Children were branded as witches by family members who believed that they embodied evil spirits and practiced witchcraft.

All unfortunate events needed to be pinned on a human being. Children were especially vulnerable to having blame placed upon them, especially if they had been the last born before the event had occurred. After her mother had died, Faith had been branded as a witch by her uncle and sent away. I continued to watch as she readied her things. When she saw me, she ran over to the gate where I was standing. Stopping short in front of me, she placed her hands upon her hips.

"Where were you?" she demanded in French.

It was four o'clock.

"*Tu m'as dites quatorze heures!*" You told me two o'clock she said. "*Je t'attendais depuis deux heures!*" I have been waiting for you for two hours!

"*Je suis désolé,*" I'm sorry, I said. I often made errors in French when using military time. "*Alors, arrange-toi tes choses, allez,*" All right, get your things, let's go, I said.

Faith stomped off to collect her belongings.

When we arrived at the orphanage, Faith refused to get out of the truck. I stepped aside as the driver—a father of six—coaxed her out. Once she was out of the truck, I took her hand, and we walked with the driver through the open courtyard. When we arrived at the door to the director's small house, we were ushered into a sitting room where the director joined us with his wife.

The director told Faith how happy that he was to see her again. After a few minutes, he asked Faith if she was ready to apologize to the boy. She said that she was. The director asked her to follow him outside. I went over to the window to watch.

Faith held out her hand to the boy as she spoke. She was humble, poised. When she had finished, the boy nodded, turned, and ran off. Faith and the director came back into the house. I thanked the director and took Faith aside. I leaned over and knelt down in front of her.

"*Tu as fait une merveilleuse chose aujourd'hui,*" You have done a wonderful thing today, I said. "*Tu es une très bonne fille.*" You are a very good girl.

I told her that the counselors that she knew from the center would come to see her early the following week. The driver and I said our good-byes. As we turned around in the rocky driveway, I tightened my grip around the handrail attached to the inside of the Land Cruiser. As we drove off, Faith stood next to the director, holding his hand. I hung onto the handrail, holding her gaze.

Before the start of the new school year, the psychosocial support team from the street children's center reunited Faith with her grandmother. The team of Congolese professionals from our staff met with Faith's grandmother, her neighbors, and local community leaders to educate them about the rights of a child. A number of sessions were held to dispel negative beliefs, which had resulted in Faith being banned from her home after her mother's death. When her grandmother was ready to accept Faith back into the family, she returned to her village.

On the appointed day, Faith arrived in her village with a reintegration package of essential items—a mattress, basic foodstuffs, a small amount of cash for school fees, and a school uniform—to aid in her transition back home.

A few months later, the program coordinator called me to update me on Faith's progress. The team from the center had recently returned from a routine follow-up visit to see Faith in her village.

"She is doing very well," the program coordinator reported. "Faith is attending school regularly, and she is first in her class."

I hung up the phone and sat back in my chair. Each day I did not leave the office without recalling at least one positive moment from my day. That day, I did not need to search far for my silver lining—Faith had returned home and she was thriving. She had made me and the other staff who had worked with her—both expatriate and Congolese—proud.

I gathered my things. I stood for a moment, absently staring down at the key after locking my office door, wishing that

Faith's mother could see her. I pulled the key out of the door and twisted the knob to ensure that the door was locked.

I passed through the office toward the front courtyard. Dusk had fallen; the sky had begun to fill with stars. Venus shone brightly in the distance. I smiled at the guard as I passed through the gate. For the first time in a long time, I was returning home with a full heart.

The next morning, I went into the bathroom and leaned over the tub. I turned on the faucet. A spattering of droplets fell onto my fingertips. I regretted not having showered the night before when the generator had been on. Water was delivered to a tank on the side of the house, where we treated it with chlorine before it was pumped inside of the house. We used a generator to light the houses, run the water pumps, and spin the fans for up to four hours each night when there was no city power. But we never ran the generator in the mornings.

I pulled the lid off of the emergency supply of water in the tall plastic bin next to the sink in the bathroom. It had not been refreshed for weeks, but the sediment had fallen to the bottom. I reached for the plastic pitcher bobbing on the top of the water. I splashed tepid water from the bin over my body—a welcome respite from the warm, humid air around me. I refilled the pitcher and poured it over my skin, cooling my back and arms. Within minutes, I would be sweating again.

I slid the patio door open and slipped through the thick blue netting used to keep the mosquitoes out. I snapped the padlock around the steel throng burrowed into the side of the house. As I turned to go around the house to the garage, my eyes were pulled into the void under the open *paiotte*. The round slab of cement flooring, positioned under the thick, grass roofing held up by poles, was empty.

I summoned the night guard. He was busily splashing water over himself in the open garage. Shirtless, he sauntered over to where I was standing, holding an empty plastic pitcher in his hand.

"Où est la table et toutes les chaises en plastiques?" Where is the plastic table and chairs? I asked.

He stared at me blankly.

"Où?" I repeated more sternly.

"Ahaahaah?" rang on his voice—a blatant lie.

There is an impressive beauty in the oral tradition of Africa as truth is pulled through the ages on the voices of generations—verbatim. A few weeks earlier, there had been a break-in at our new guesthouse. The thief had climbed over the neighboring fence, anchoring his foot on the wide berth of the air conditioner attached to the outside wall of one of the second-floor bedrooms. He had dropped down and tried to slip into the back door when he had been seen by the guard. The thief had slipped through the front gate and he had run, but not before he had grabbed the radio next to the guard station. The guard had chased him down the street, but the thief had escaped.

Recounted word-for-word by three staff waiting excitedly outside my door the following morning before I left for the office, the story had remained intact. Once I arrived at the office, there was a line of staff waiting to recount it to me yet again.

I bristled past the guard and made my way to the garage. The guard was still standing on the side of the house as I yelled for him to open the gate. When I reached the office compound, I called the guard supervisor into my office to report the theft.

When I was finished, the guard supervisor assured me that he would undertake a thorough investigation. Before the end of the day, he returned to my office with a full report.

"*Directrice*," Boss, he said. He looked down at his notes. "*Un voleur a pris les choses pendant la nuit tandis que les gardes dormaient.*" A thief took the items during the night while the guards were sleeping.

He offered up proof. A black smudge had been left by the thief as he had climbed over the exterior wall to escape with the stolen goods.

I stood up and planted my fingers on the top of my desk.

"Well, then," I said in French, "we should fire the guards for sleeping during their night shift."

He looked back at me and then down at his notes before sputtering, "*Mais, Directrice, ce n'était pas leur faute!*" But Boss, it was not their fault!

I raised my arm and pointed to the door of my office.

"Get out!" I shouted in English.

It was the first time that I had lost my temper with any of the staff. In later years, during evacuations and other serious security incidents, I would yell out of frustration, with worry, to punctuate directions with immediacy. But that day in Brazzaville I was angry.

The guard supervisor turned and left.

That evening, I did not greet the guards. I pulled the small rental car that I drove back and forth to the office through the gates of the garage, got out, and walked around the house. Unlocking the padlock, I slid the heavy door open, entered the house, and slammed the door shut behind me.

I searched the cupboards in the kitchen for an industrial flashlight. I found one in the metal container where we stored a ten-day emergency stock of dried goods, bottled water, and candles to be used in the event of a lockdown. I pulled the flashlight out of the steel locker and flipped it on. The batteries were good.

As I approached the door to the patio, I slid it open, stepped through it, turned, and slammed it shut. The two guards stationed at my house for the night shift stood off to the side of the house. The two guards stationed at the guesthouse next door looked in through the entryway that we had cut into the wall between the two houses.

Without a word, I lifted the flashlight into the air and turned it on. I walked to the back of the yard, pointing the flashlight at the top of the eight-foot wall. I walked inside the perimeter of the compound, shining the light over the top of the wall. When I got to the front of the yard, I turned the flashlight off and set it on the ground.

I looked at one of the guards.

"Where is the foot mark that was left by the thief?" I demanded in French.

The guard who was standing closest to me pointed at a small, black smudge shoulder-height on the cement wall in front of him. The smudge was the size of my fingernail.

"*Regardez, Directrice, c'est ici!*" Look, Boss, here it is! he said.

There were two plastic chairs under the *paiotte*. The guards had pulled them from the garage where they had slept on them the night before. I grabbed one of the plastic chairs and dragged it out from under the *paiotte*. I picked it up and threw it over the high wall in front of me.

"Did you hear that?" I yelled in French.

I stomped over to the pedestrian gate next to the garage and opened the metal door. I went outside, picked up the chair from the dirt road outside of the house, and threw it back over the wall. I came back in through the gate.

"Did you hear that?" I screamed again in French.

I leaned over, picked up the flashlight, and stomped back into the house, once again slamming the door behind me.

I did not speak to the guards for three days. Prior to the incident, I had been close to many of them. My guards were my first line of defense. I joked with them, shared food with them, ensured that they had fair salaries and benefits. And, unless they proved otherwise, I trusted them.

On the third day, one of the guards approached me and asked if he could speak to me. He said that he had information on the case. I agreed.

We stood outside of the house on the patio in front of the door. As he spoke, he looked down at the cement flooring. He told me that he had located the table and chairs. They were at the house on the corner in the home of Lieutenant Davie.

"He heard something in the night and went out into the street where he saw a thief running," the guard recounted in French. "When the thief saw him, he dropped the table and chairs in the middle of the street and ran off into the night."

I waited.

"Lieutenant Davie has the table and chairs," he continued. "He said that he would sell them back to you."

I took a deep breath, but I did not have the patience to count to ten.

"Je vais lui demander de me rendre mes choses," I'm going to ask him to give my things back to me, I said. *"Et, je ne vais pas les acheter."* And, I am not going to buy them.

This was clearly not what my guard had expected to hear. He raised his eyes from the pavement and stood staring at me.

"Or, you can tell Lieutenant Davie that he has stolen goods that are the property of the US government, purchased with US government funds," I continued in French. "And I will be forced to inform the US ambassador if he does not return them immediately."

I went back into the house.

Later that day, the table and chairs reappeared under the *paiotte*. When I went out that evening, I saw that they had been neatly arranged in their proper place. I suspected that the guards had had to buy them back from Lieutenant Davie. I knew that there was a slim possibility that the items had initially been commandeered, but it was more probable that the guards had simply sold them. I had no way of knowing. I was only certain that they had not been stolen.

After I had been in Brazzaville for a year, I was told that the national staff had a tally board of all of the expatriates who had worked for the organization over the previous two years. There had been over one hundred names etched in chalk on a board in the radio room. Many of the expatriates, including key senior staff, had stayed for extremely short periods, causing frustration and confusion as the national staff weathered a constant barrage of changing policies, procedures, and management styles.

When I asked the radio operator if I could see the board, he smiled broadly. He told me that he was no longer keeping tally. There was no need. He had erased the long list of names when none of the current team of expatriates had left their posts after six months.

A number of new international staff had been hired prior to my arrival a year before. I had taken over management of the country program with a new team. I had spent the first nine months building up the expatriate team, providing training and mentoring to the newer international staff—an investment that had paid off. I was happy to learn that the chalkboard had been erased. It meant that the national staff took the current expatriate team seriously.

I held out my hand, and the radio operator grasped it.

"Thanks so much for the great work that you do," I said in French. "Thanks also for trusting me. It means a lot."

"*Merci, Madame la Directrice*," Thank you, Boss, he said shyly.

He was one of the most professional and dependable national colleagues that I had worked with in Brazzaville. My initial months had been difficult. Some of the senior national staff had not been trustworthy. I had had many suspicions, but was rarely able to adequately prove wrongdoing.

One day, I had pulled a member of the logistics staff into my office to investigate a case of corruption, thinking that he had been involved as the ringleader. The following day, I learned that I had been wrong. I asked to talk to my colleague again. We were standing next to the back door near the outdoor courtyard as I looked him in the eye.

"I'm sorry," I said in French. "I was wrong."

He stared back at me as I spoke. When I was finished, he reached out his hand to shake mine. Although his eyes conveyed gratitude, his voice remained silent. It was the first time that he had received an apology from a supervisor.

I had been taught well. When I was younger, my father had become angry with me, but I had not understood why. Later, my father had apologized. I had felt a deep sense of relief after my father's apology, but it was the deep sense of respect that I had felt for my father that day that had stayed with me.

During my second year in Brazzaville, with the help of a strong group of international colleagues, I began to build the capacity of the national staff. I held all of my colleagues in Brazzaville to a high professional standard, expecting as much out of them as I expected out of myself. As a result, we became a solid team.

Some months later, during a regional meeting in Nairobi, I was standing at the bar enjoying a drink with a group of colleagues from the regional office. A member of the international finance team joined us, and I was introduced as the new country director in Brazzaville.

"Oh, you're the new CD in Brazza," the finance staff member said upon meeting me. "Your country program is doing very well. You're off of the black list."

I looked back at her, not knowing what to say. I had not known that there was a black list. I only knew that we no longer needed to buy chalk in bulk.

I traveled extensively to the field, strapping on a fanny pack each time that I prepared to board a UN flight to fly out of the capital. Around my waist, I carried a flashlight, tissues, and extra batteries. And I never traveled without water.

I was often invited to sit next to the English-speaking pilot as we sputtered over the equator in a single-engine aircraft. The day I turned forty-four years old, I learned what the *AP* light on the airplane console meant. When I mentioned to the pilot that it was my birthday, he grabbed his camera, jumped up from his seat, and walked to the back of the small plane. My eyes grew wide as I twisted my body toward the back of the aircraft. I was traveling with a colleague. He stared back at me, his eyes larger and wider than mine.

"Don't worry," the pilot said. "The plane is on automatic pilot."

"What?" I asked.

"We've been on automatic pilot since we crossed the equator," he said. "Look on the console."

I turned and looked for the small light that he had described to me. It was illuminated.

Still strapped in, I twisted around awkwardly in my seat. The pilot was crouched over in the rear of the small aircraft, holding a camera up to his eye.

"Smile!" he said.

Weeks later, I was traveling on the same airplane with a different pilot. Sitting next to the pilot while I read, I noticed his head bob out of the corner of my eye. So as not to alert the other passengers, I didn't poke him. Instead, I pulled my body forward in my seat and coughed loudly. He woke up. I smiled, sat back, and continued to read.

Our field site was in a remote area in the north of the country along the Ubangi River. The red-clay dirt runway, cleared out of the forest by an Italian logging company, often became saturated after the rains. When this happened, the small plane soared to its next destination after circling the runway without landing, leaving the passengers on the manifest of the aborted flight stranded for days.

The forest was so fertile and lush that foliage grew up to three feet or more between site visits. Because our programs included water and sanitation activities, whenever I traveled to the field, I had access to clean water. The showers and latrines, however, were outdoors. Tall rubber boots—necessary to get from one area of the compound to another during heavy rains—were hedged against the walls of each hut.

In the early evenings, we sat outside as bats swooped too close to our heads. Industrial flashlights, attached to the corners of poles holding up the grass roofing over the outdoor sitting area, attracted hundreds of giant moths—their wings fluttering against the bulbs, further dimming the weak light that spilled out around them.

We stayed in small huts on a compound that we had constructed from the ground up. We ate meals in a communal hut. A single bulb, hanging from the center of the grass roofing inside of the hut, provided illumination when the generator was running. When the generator was turned off to conserve fuel, we lit candles and sat alongside wide shadows, cast onto the brick walls around us by the stark light.

After dinner we sat drinking beer as we discussed a long list of management and coordination issues late into the night. Each time that I traveled out to the field, I arranged one-on-one meetings with key national and expatriate staff to check-in and confirm individual commitments to stay on with the team. In time, we prepared the refugee population to return to their villages across the river, and our work in the country was completed.

When I was new to humanitarian aid work, I wondered if displaced populations ever returned home. There was a reason that the refugees had stayed so long in the villages along the river. They had access to basic health care. Education was provided for their children. They were provided with essential food and non-food items. Until basic services became available, and they were safely able to plant and harvest crops in their fields on the other side of the river, the refugees had not been interested in leaving.

Some of the refugees had inter-married. They had started families or businesses in their host villages along the river. Yet, no matter how deeply they planted roots after fleeing their country, something inside of them continued to tug at them— eventually pulling them back home.

ONE HUNDRED MINUTES

How shall I measure that which is not mine?
The flick of a wrist, the blink of an eye
Sell me the ripening fruit off the vine,
One hundred minutes of time I shall buy.
My dreams bring to light life's riddles in rhyme,
My days full of wonder end with a sigh,
One thought a penny, life turns on a dime,
One hundred minutes of time I shall buy.
How shall I purchase this gift so divine?
My pockets empty as hard as I try
The world is my banquet, water my wine,
One hundred minutes of time I shall buy.
Each beat of my heart a star in the sky,
Each passing moment a minute gone by.

Brazzaville, Republic of Congo, 2005

CÔTE D'IVOIRE

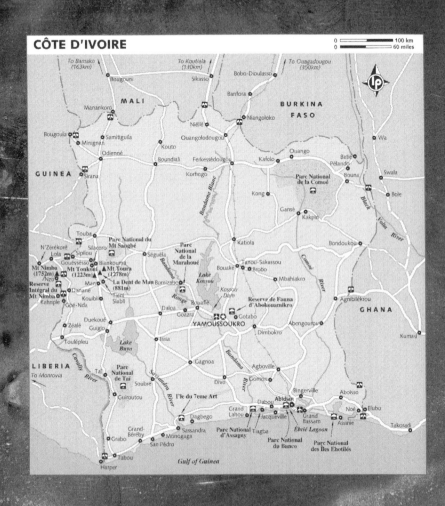

Chapter Ten

PIT STOP IN THE PARIS OF AFRICA

Abidjan 2005

The phone rang. I rolled over and reached onto the floor beside the bed. Pulling the phone up to my ear, I pushed the button to receive the call.

"Hello?"

"Are you okay?" a male voice asked. "Do you need me to get you out?"

The cadence of Paul's voice was soothing.

"Hi," I said as I sat up in bed.

The situation was extremely tense. University students had taken to the streets with funding from the president to intimidate expatriates in Abidjan. Two Air France flights had been diverted from landing due to the violence on the ground.

The day before, I had been in communication with my colleagues in the field, other international agencies, and my home office. The calls had come in steadily throughout the day—updates from security sources and check-ins from the field—until I had fallen into bed late into the night, hungry and exhausted.

"I'm fine, thanks, but I may need to ask you to extract one of my colleagues from the field."

As soon as I said the words, I wished that I could take them back—this was not what had been offered. His company was a

for-profit business. I had other options. I could work through
the United Nations Humanitarian Air Service or the French
military if I needed to extract one of my staff from the field.

I had only known Paul for a few months. I had met him at
a security training where he had taught me how to punch out
a car. We had much in common, including an interest in communications and neurolinguistic programming. I had also been
a trainer. Knowing how difficult that it was to keep a group of
participants engaged, I was impressed at the level of energy he
brought to his work. He also had an incredible sense of humor.

"Thanks so much for calling," I said. I needed to go; the
daily check-in calls from the field sites were scheduled to begin.

"Call me if you need me," he said.

"I will, I promise."

"Remember," he said. "I'm only a flight away."

I had been in the capital of Cote d'Ivoire for less than three
months, when an open position in Chad prompted the home
office to call me. Someone was needed to help the regional
office get the program back on track. I was asked to fill in on
an interim basis. I knew, however, that once I departed I would
not return. We had two strong senior staff in Abidjan, there
was a need in Chad, and I loved the desert.

Before the war, Abidjan had been known as the Paris of
Africa. Following independence in 1960, the country continued to benefit from international investment. The capital had
hi-rise buildings, five-star hotels, upscale shops, and high-end
restaurants. But in 2002, a civil war divided the nation. When
I arrived, the UN was monitoring the fragile peace along the
east-west buffer zone that cut across the country.

The country program had been without leadership for a number of months. A strong and competent deputy director was sent in to work with me. Together, we rolled up our sleeves and addressed many outstanding management issues, stabilizing the program. The deputy director worked well with the team to expand programming after the emergency response. He attracted new avenues of funding. As I prepared to leave, I was confident that the program would be well managed by the team in Abidjan. I was needed in Chad.

Very soon after receiving the phone call from the home office, I left the Paris of Africa and flew halfway across the continent. Arriving in a small, dusty town in the middle of the desert, I had happily left the uncomfortably humid climate of Abidjan behind. The plane landed and I made my way to the open door leading down to the tarmac. I stopped for a moment at the top of the stairway to pull in a hot, dry, dusty breath of air. I began my descent. I had missed living in the desert.

TRANSLUCENT THUNDER

Each passing moment marks eternity
Empty, the space between two sparks a blast.
Hope floating freely from future to past,
Mist from your vapor breathes life into me.
Unleash the meaning of all that is one
Shrouded in fear in a dark corner room
Shielded from sunlight, sharp crackle—KA-BOOM!
Cuts through the clouds, clears a path to the sun.
Falling from heaven once cool waters burst,
Easing the threat as catastrophe wanes,
Deep-seated thunder sparks choral refrains,
Lost souls—lone molecules—no longer thirst.
Translucent thunder cracks open the dome,
Mist swirling silver, our souls return home.

Abidjan, Cote d'Ivoire, 2005

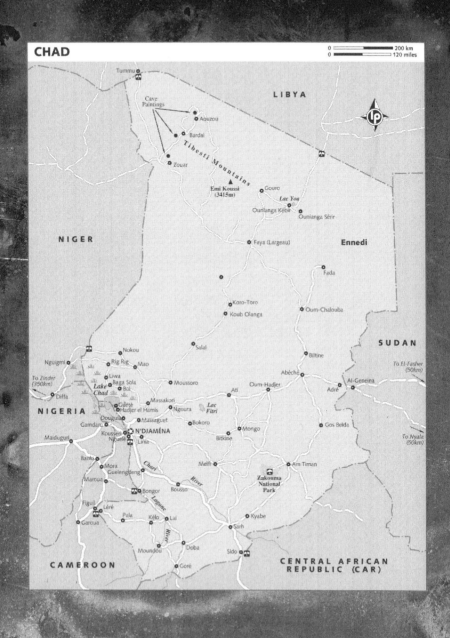

CHAD

0 ———————— 200 km
0 ———————— 120 miles

LIBYA

Tummu

Cave Paintings

Aouzou

Bardaï

Tibesti Mountains

Zouar

Emi Koussi (3415m) ▲

Gouro

Lac Yoa

Ounianga Kébir

Ounianga Sérir

NIGER

Faya (Largeau)

Ennedi

Fada

Koro-Toro

Koub Olanga

Oum-Chalouba

SUDAN

Nokou

Salal

Biltine

To El-Fasher (50km)

Nguigmi

Rig Rig

Mao

Abéché

Al-Geneina

To Zinder (350km)

Liwa

Baga Sola

Bol

Moussoro

Ati

Oum-Hadjer

Adré

Diffa

Lake Chad

Gaété

Massakori

Ngoura

Lac Fitri

NIGERIA

Hadjer el Hamis

Dougula

Massaguet

Bokoro

Mongo

Gos Beïda

To Nyala (50km)

Gamdam

Koussen

N'DJAMÉNA

Linia

Bitkine

Maiduguri

Nguele

Chari

Melfi

Am Timan

Banlo

Mora

Guelengdeng

River

Bousso

Zakouma National Park

Maroua

Bongor

Figuil

Léré

Pala

Kélo

Laï

Kyabe

Garoua

River

Doba

Sido

Moundou

CENTRAL AFRICAN REPUBLIC (CAR)

Goré

CAMEROON

Sarh

Chapter Eleven

THE COLOR OF NIGHT

Abeche 2006

I was crossing the dirt road from my office to the staff compound, carrying a mattress on my back. Neil was tinkering in his truck with his radio. A former pilot, he monitored the humanitarian air traffic in Abeche from his vehicle. He was older than most of the humanitarian aid workers. And, like me, he had an appreciation for German cars. That night, I tagged along with Neil and another colleague to a party.

The following week, when I flew to the capital for a meeting, I ran into Neil at the airport. It was five o'clock in the morning. A cigarette hung out of the corner of his mouth as he weighed my luggage. Due to the security situation, we had not been able to travel by road for months. Small aircraft was our only means of transportation. UN flights enforced a strict weight limit, allowing no more than fifteen kilos per passenger. I traveled with ten kilos stuffed into a small suitcase and another five kilos in my computer bag.

"I'll be at the airport to meet you when you return next week," he said. "Oh, and I need your number since you will be the new director, for emergency purposes."

He pulled out his phone. The passengers were walking across the tarmac toward the plane. Many already had boarded the aircraft.

"I don't know my number," I said. "I need to check the phone my colleague gave me."

"Don't worry," he said. "The plane won't leave without you. Come on, I'll drive you out."

As I climbed into his truck, the radio crackled. Neil pulled the mouthpiece off of the dash.

"Roger that, the runway has already been cleared," he said. "I have one more passenger in the truck with me. I'm bringing her out to the plane now. Over."

He snapped the mouthpiece back onto the metal hook attached to the dashboard, grabbed the transmission stick, and put the truck into gear.

Rebels roamed the dusty streets of Abeche, a small desert town located midway along the border with the state of West Darfur in neighboring Sudan. Each morning, tanks rolled out of the nearby military encampment to conduct exercises when they were not being deployed along the border. International organizations had stopped using pickup trucks following a rash of vehicle thefts in the city, opting instead to travel in small, unmarked rental cars. Roadblocks, open conflict, and attempted coups were frequent during the dry season. Insecurity continued through the rainy season unless there were particularly heavy rains.

As a child, I grew up with four distinct seasons. In Africa, there were two—the rainy season and the dry season. In some countries, there were two more—the little rainy season and the little dry season. Before the rains, lush foliage along the equator became clay-like—red in color, chalky in texture—until the rains arrived to cleanse the earth. Near the capital, small patches of green earth could be seen during takeoff from the international airport. The desert, which was half of the country and all of the north, remained beige year-round.

From the air, everything was flat. Makeshift roads shifted with the sands. Heavy rains fell in sheets, cutting rivers into the earth in seemingly senseless directions. Torrential waters flowed out of nowhere, taking Land Cruisers on wild rides through otherwise dry, crusty ravines.

My house had four walls, three rooms, and two ceiling fans. A large screened-in porch was attached to the back side of the house. A small kitchen area, with a hotplate, was located at one end of the porch. A large bathroom, with an open bucket shower, was located on the other end. I stepped over six-inch-high moldings of plywood covered in cement to enter the porch from the house.

A hole drilled through the cement molding along the wall of the porch, was used to push water out of the room after cleaning the cement floor. Slipping in through the hole, a black mouse entered the house each night like clockwork. After circling the porch, it ran into the kitchen before buckling back along the molding each evening at dusk. Swarms of bugs fluttered around my head at night as I tried to read under the stark bulb above my bed. Marking time with their short-lived lives, their transparent wings lay in piles of near-dust on the windowsill each morning—only to be swept away to make room for a new breed, hatched before dawn.

Next to my house was the staff compound, where the other international staff lived. Colleagues from other field sites also stayed there when they came into Abeche for technical meetings or when traveling through on their way out of the country for R&R.

There was no city power. The office was powered by a generator. It was shut off for two hours in the afternoon and two hours in the early morning. There was no air conditioning.

We ran cheap plastic fans we had bought from the market while we slept. There was no running water. We dug wells or trucked water to the compound for our daily needs.

I asked the logistics team to construct walkways between the sleeping rooms and the latrines. When I had arrived, my colleagues were living in what appeared to be a giant sandbox. An elaborate design for the cement walkways was proposed by a local contractor. The list of necessary materials was reviewed and revised before a contract was signed. Melting with the first rains as a result of poor quality standards, reconstruction required a full-time foreman to oversee the work before any final invoices were paid.

Neil slipped the key out of the inside lock of the door on the side of my house.

"I'll hold on to this for emergencies," he said.

He was burrowing his way into my life. I initially had not wanted him to be close to me. I fiercely guarded my freedom. He persisted. With time, I learned that by being with him, I could gain more freedom. And, I could have much more fun. I began to relax. Neil understood what I was going through. He knew what I needed. Until I met Neil, I had only relied on myself when I had been out in the bush. In Chad, I allowed my life to change.

I received a message from the home office. The team in communications was working with a celebrity who was trying to get into Darfur. He was slated to speak at a rally in Washington, DC, and he wanted to talk with the displaced populations in the region. He wasn't able to obtain a visa for Sudan, so he asked to travel to Chad to meet with the refugees along the border.

There had been a number of troop movements up and down the border area. We were under lockdown in Abeche from dusk to dawn. I would be able to charter a private plane through a French pilot that I knew. He had flown another celebrity to at least two of the camps two years earlier. But there would be issues getting the celebrity into the country, and he would be traveling with his father.

I had arranged to fly back to the US for a wedding. The timing coincided with the arrival of the celebrity. I worked through all of the details in concert with the senior management team. Once the arrangements had been made, I informed the home office that I would not be on the ground when the celebrity arrived. I wrote the e-mail and pushed *send*.

That night I couldn't sleep. How many times had I forgone spending the Christmas holidays with my family for the sake of my work? How many weddings had I missed? How many family dinners, birthday parties, or anniversary celebrations had I attended as a ghost? I had planned on going home for the wedding of my youngest sister for months. But I was the country director, and the home office would be counting on me to ensure that the logistics on the ground were well managed during the celebrity visit. What happened on the ground in Chad was my responsibility, and whether or not I was in country, I would be held accountable.

I called the vice president the next day to retract my decision. I said that I would forgo my leave and stay in Chad for the duration of the celebrity visit.

"I am happy to hear that," was the reply.

The damage already had been done. Prior to that day, I had been the go-to girl—I was the cleaner, happily going into country programs that were struggling. I rolled up my sleeves and pulled disparate teams together without complaint. I sought out these challenges, believing that smaller programs often needed the greatest amount of attention. But my initial decision had been my demise. I had lost credibility with the home office when I had put my personal life before my work.

I continued with the logistical preparations for the visit. A conference call with the celebrity and his father was scheduled. The senior management team would be on the call with me, the celebrity, and his father. I also expected that a number of other staff would be listening in. The call was arranged during the morning hours in the US. In my time zone, it was six in the evening.

Curfew was approaching. I checked my e-mail, clicking on a message from my brother. He wanted me to know that my mother was in the intensive care unit at the hospital. She had had an issue with her heart that had deteriorated the day before. My mother's doctor had called the family into the hospital to say their good-byes.

My mother had never had trouble with her heart before. I thought of the few times in my childhood that she had fallen ill as a result of overwork. More than once, pneumonia had forced her to stop and rest when nothing else had been able to slow her down.

I closed my laptop and looked out of the window of my small office. In less than an hour, I would be on the phone with the celebrity and his father. I needed to decide if I was going to call home before or after the conference call.

I was in the middle of the desert. To get home, I would need to fly to the capital on a UN flight before I could transfer to an international airline. The shortest amount of time to travel from Abeche to Minneapolis would be four days.

I called my brother.

"Mom is doing better," he said.

The family was at her side. She had regained her strength during the night.

Neil arrived to take me home.

"Thanks for letting me know, Teddy," I said. "I'm sorry, but I really have to go."

As Neil and I approached his compound, the guard opened the gate. Before we entered, the guard put his arm up, signaling us to wait. The metal gate closed. When the gate reopened the guard was leaning over, holding onto the thin horns of the springbok adopted by the pilots who lived in the house. He had been running through the dusty streets of Abeche when Neil had found him.

His legs slim, his movements agile, he often slipped out of the gate when vehicles entered the compound. When this happened, the guards ran into the road, crossing the street into an open lot. Running in circles, the springbok dodged the guards, kicking up wafts of dust under his small hooves as the guards grabbed at his sharp horns.

Once inside, I asked Neil to update me on any issues related to air travel. I had confirmed the chartered plane earlier that day, outlining alternative routes with the pilot. I had met with the senior staff to draft a security briefing. I gathered my notes and went outside with the satellite phone. I opened the door to Neil's truck and leaned against the side of the front seat. I pointed the antennae of the satellite phone toward the sky, moving it at various angles until I had five bars of reception. It was dark, but the numbers on the keypad were illuminated in a soft, yellow-gold light. I dialed the number and punched in the conference code for the call. I was greeted by a roomful of home office staff. We added the celebrity's father to the call.

"How are you?" I asked.

His voice was warm but gruff. "My arm hurts," he said.

I laughed. "What happened?" I asked.

"I got all these damn shots today," he replied.

We needed to wait; the celebrity's people were still arranging for him to take the call. They were calling from his office, which was near one of the lots in Hollywood where he had had a meeting earlier that day. I looked up at the stars. The Southern Cross, my favorite constellation, hung low along the horizon, threatening to slip away.

"Don't worry, you'll feel better soon," I said to the celebrity's father. "The pain from the yellow fever shot is sharp at first, but it'll go away by the end of the day."

"A shot of Maker's Mark should do the trick," he said.

"He's ready, he's here, let's go," an unknown voice barked into the phone.

There was a pause.

"Hello?"

I recognized the voice.

"Hi, everyone, sorry I'm late," the voice continued.

A senior staff member from the home office welcomed the celebrity to the call. I was asked to give a briefing.

"Hi, everyone," I said. "I'm going to give you an update on what's happening here on the ground and then we can talk about some options."

When I had finished with the briefing, the celebrity commented on the situation in the region. He was well versed on the issues on both sides of the border. In my work, I only focused on the area of operation that I was managing.

"I know that you're not going to want to hear this, but there have been some troop movements that may not allow you to come into the country as planned," I said. "There's talk of a coup in the capital. We should know within a few days if you can come out or not."

I provided context on the living arrangements in the remote site that the celebrity and his father would be visiting.

"There's one thing that I think that you should know," I said. "The site where you'll be staying is very remote, and it's not very comfortable."

We had built a rudimentary compound with twenty small rooms, each with a cot. The staff shared two latrines and two outdoor showers, located at the far end of the compound. Each day, the temperatures hovered around one hundred and ten degrees Fahrenheit. In the evenings during the dry season, the temperature only dropped to ninety degrees. In the rainy season, it became cold at night.

"No problem," the celebrity said. "I spent a few days with a couple of buddies in the desert once."

I had seen the movie he had filmed in the desert. I imagined the fully stocked trailer with air conditioning that he had no doubt returned to after shooting each scene. There would be no trailers where he was going.

"Okay, good," I said. "I have to say, from the bottom of my heart, we all appreciate what you are doing."

"When I won my Oscar," he said, "my father told me that I needed to use my celebrity for the greater good."

"Well, then we're lucky," I said. "The refugees need someone with your stature to give voice to their issues. Thank you so much."

He needed to go.

"Good-bye, everyone," he said. "Good-bye, Pop."

His father was asked to stay on the line to finalize logistics for the trip.

"Well, somebody's going to hear it from me if we're not able to go out there because of a coup," the celebrity's father said. It was the first time that he had spoken since his son had joined the call. "I already got these damn shots!" he added.

For the second time that day, I laughed.

"It's nothing that a bottle of Maker's Mark won't take care of," I said, "but, I'm a Bushies girl, myself."

I sensed silent gasps on the other end of the line as my colleagues listened to the banter. Although my colleagues—

especially the women—were excited to meet the celebrity, I was more interested in meeting his father. I was happily living with Neil. The management of the logistics for the celebrity visit was my job, but I also knew that his father had been the one to encourage his son to travel to the region. I admired him for it, and wanted the opportunity to sit and talk with him about his life over a glass of whiskey.

The next day, I called my mother. She told me that she was feeling better; her blood pressure had stabilized. We laughed together as I recounted the conversation that I had had with the celebrity and his father.

"Do you know how proud of you that I am?" she asked.

"Mom, come on," I said.

"I understand how his father feels. It's important to support your children even if they go somewhere you don't want them to go," she said. "I think it's admirable that his father is going out to Chad with him."

"Me too, Mom," I said.

Over the following days, my mother's condition improved. I was in touch with her every day as I continued to monitor the security situation in preparation for the celebrity's visit.

"I spoke to my mother," I said during my daily management call with the home office. "She is doing much better."

The senior team was concerned that I would not be able to keep my focus if my mother's condition took a turn for the worse. An emergency staff member was appointed to take over for me. I was free to go home.

I was sitting in my mother's bedroom, talking with her as she rested. In the background, Oprah came on to promote her daytime talk show.

"Today, we will be speaking with a celebrity who has just returned from a place that is so secret he can't even tell you where he's been." The promo rang on, "Next! On Oprah."

I looked over at my mother.

"I know where he was," I said.

When the celebrity came on, he discussed his findings and showed footage and photographs of the remote site where he and his father had met with the refugees. The dust swirled over his head as he stood in the open pickup truck, filming. He had fallen ill while he was away. I wondered about his father.

"I should have been there, Mom," I said. "I bet he drank the water at the site. I don't even do that."

I had intended to preposition cases of water for the celebrity and his father. I wondered if my directive had fallen through the cracks.

Two weeks later, I returned to Abeche. As I stood at the top of the stairs leading down to the tarmac, Neil pulled up alongside the plane. He jumped out of his truck and walked briskly to the window under the cockpit of the plane to speak to the pilots. I had seen his blue truck at the end of the runway as we had descended into Abeche. He was waiting on a small, dusty hill at the same point on the runway where the plane had touched down.

Small, round *tukels*, grass huts, housed a number of families dangerously close to the airport. It was not uncommon for their cattle to walk onto the runway as they grazed. There was no fencing between their land and the runway. Neil had traveled the runway before the plane had landed to rid it of any stray animals.

As the pilot pulled the luggage out of the back of the plane, Neil walked over and kissed me. He had left his truck running, with the air-conditioner on, so that it would be cool when I arrived. He told me to get into the truck as he walked around the plane. He pulled my suitcase out of the pile of luggage that was being loaded into the back of a pickup truck. I climbed into the front seat of his truck, sat back, and let the cool air flow over me, happy to be home.

A few weeks later, a colleague from the home office who had traveled with the celebrity and his father sent me a file of the photos she had taken during the visit. Later that day, I received a separate message with a single photo. I clicked on the attachment. In the photograph, two men stood squinting into the sun. One was wearing a flap jacket, the other a smile. I leaned in closer to read the handwritten message on the piece of paper that they were holding up between them: *Julie, wish you were here.*

Expatriates traveled out of the country every eight to twelve weeks depending on the R&R benefit in their contracts. When we were together in Chad, Neil was overly attentive. While he was away, he was out of touch.

After we had been living together for some months, Neil accepted a lateral transfer to a neighboring country. He asked me how I felt about it. I told him that by accepting the transfer, he had decided the future of our relationship. Two weeks later, he was gone.

When he left Chad, I didn't expect to see him again. We had arranged to go sailing with a group of friends in the Adriatic. I went alone. Three of the people on the sailboat were on R&R from their work in the same area where Neil had been transferred. It was Neil's birthday, and I imagined him sitting alone in a hotel in Nairobi waiting for a visa, which could take weeks to obtain.

We were in a cove swimming when I pulled myself back onto the boat. I had brought my satellite phone along in case my staff needed to contact me while I was away. Through my extended networks, I found Neil. He was at home. When I called his number, a woman answered. She passed the phone to Neil, and he pretended that he didn't know who I was. Some years later, when I was preparing to fly into Somalia, I went to the UN office in Nairobi to confirm my flight. One of the administrators had been with Neil in his previous post. I asked how he was.

"You haven't heard?"

"No," I replied.

"Neil died a few months ago," he said.

He hadn't felt well so he had left the airport early one day. "It was very sad," he said. "He had recently married his long-time girlfriend."

"Thanks for telling me," I said. "I was a very close friend of his."

For years, I had asked about Neil whenever I had traveled in the region—with no result. A few weeks after I learned that he had died, I was in Sudan on business. I had carried a personal item to a woman in Khartoum as a favor to a colleague. We met for dinner.

She was with her fiancé, a pilot, and his friend who also worked for the air service. Both men knew Neil. When I told them who I was and that I had worked in Chad, the friend of the pilot said that he had heard about me. He said that he was a close friend of Neil's new wife. I asked him to give Neil's wife my condolences.

The man shot me a disdainful glance.

"Please," I said. "Look me in the eyes."

Reluctantly, he looked over at me.

"Please tell her that I didn't know, and I am very sorry for her loss."

When the details of his secret were revealed, Neil was gone for a second time.

A few months before I left Chad, I called Paul to ask him if he would be interested in conducting defensive driver training for my staff. Stationed in the far north of the country near Libya, we had had a rash of vehicle thefts. I couldn't afford to pay him his usual fees, so he flew out as a volunteer for a week to conduct the training course.

I arranged for him to fly on a UN flight to the remote area where he would be conducting the training. I remained in the capital, managing an ongoing string of security issues. Upon landing on the open airstrip, when no one had been there to greet him, Paul hitched a ride with another international organization. After driving through the desert on makeshift roads, he had been dumped at the gates of our compound.

It wasn't until he was on his way out of the country that he mentioned that I had neglected to set up an airport pickup for him. We were standing next to each other at the bar of an outdoor restaurant in the capital. It was the only time that we had managed to be alone during the week he had spent in Chad.

"What?" I said aghast. "No!"

"Yes," he said.

"No!" I repeated.

He smiled and nodded. "Yes."

"Paul, I'm so sorry," I said. "Really, you were so great to come out here to help me. I'm really, really sorry."

We were awaiting the arrival of the friends and colleagues I had invited to my farewell dinner. The first two arrived. I called the bartender over, and asked him to serve them whatever they wanted to drink. A few minutes later, the others arrived. The bartender served them each a drink.

When we had finished our aperitif, I invited everyone to join me at the table that had been set out for us under the stars. The Africans at the table ordered the camel meat. I was told it was a delicacy. I ordered it as well. After he had noted everyone's order, the waiter walked across the wide, open yard back toward the kitchen as I looked around the table.

"I want to thank you all for coming," I said. "I've really enjoyed working with you all and I really can't thank you all enough for your commitment and support over the past year."

I looked to my left. A Canadian man who worked for the air service was sitting next to me. Before Neil had left, the Canadian man had spent a lot of time with us. We had become friends.

"I want to welcome our newest colleague tonight," I said. "You have done so much for our organization already, and you have been here for only a few months. Thank you."

He nodded.

I moved my gaze to the Chadian woman sitting next to him. Near to me in age, she was the administrator in the capital responsible for managing the guesthouse.

"You are so wonderful to work with. Thank you for the support that you've provided to me and the entire staff," I said. "More than a colleague, you were a trusted cultural advisor."

A charm shaped out of the borders of Chad hung from a gold chain around my neck. I touched the necklace with my right hand.

"Thank you for this beautiful gift," I said. "When I leave tomorrow, I will take a piece of your country with me. I will remember you always. Thank you."

I continued my tour around the table, thanking each person until only two people remained. Before I spoke to the field coordinator, I stopped and took a breath.

"I have worked with so many field coordinators over the years," I said. "You have outshone them all. I was always so confident knowing that you were in charge out in the field."

I looked over at Paul.

"How lucky am I that you are with me tonight?" I asked. "I am so happy that you are here. Thank you so much for coming out to help us."

The waiter walked across the yard with three plates lodged on his arms. Another man trailed behind him. The two men returned to the table again, laden with plates. When everyone at the table had a meal in front of him or her, we raised our glasses in a toast.

"*Bon Appétit, tout le monde,*" Enjoy your meal everybody, I said.

"*Bon Voyage, A bientôt!*" they said. Have a good trip, until we meet again!

We raised our glasses a second time.

SONNET FOR SARDO

As long as planes can soar and trains can sear
Upon the crumbling archways of stone walls,
As friends pass through our lives they disappear,
As autumn glimmers gold, as new snow falls.
Release a single bullet from your heart,
Lay down to rest past lives as death would do,
Lost friends remembered as they each depart
Upon the bloodied tide of sunset's hue.
The depth within your eyes tells stories bold,
Beyond belief to some, I understand.
Cracked bones beneath my skin reach out to hold
The sinews of your heart within my hand.
As long as planes can soar and trains can sear,
Reflected in the night, I will be near.

Rome, Italy, 2012

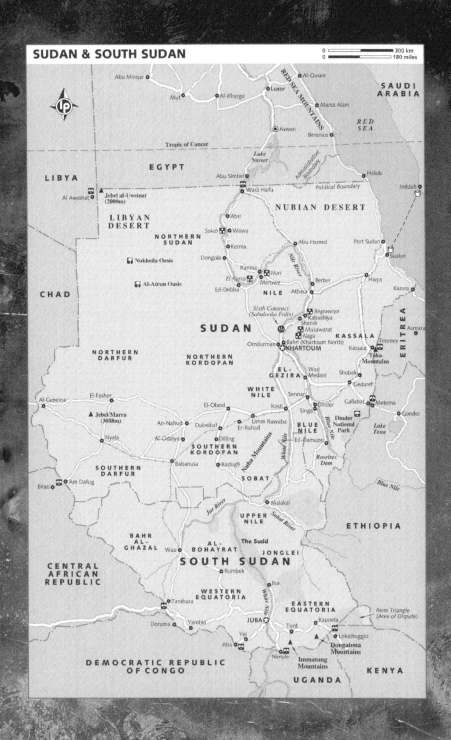

SUDAN & SOUTH SUDAN

0 — 300 km
0 — 180 miles

SAUDI ARABIA

Abu Minqar
Mut
Al-Kharga
Luxor
Al-Quseir
Marsa Alam

RED SEA MOUNTAINS

Aswan
Berenice

RED SEA

Tropic of Cancer
Lake Nasser

EGYPT

Administrative Boundary

Halaib
Jeddah

Abu Simbel
Wadi Halfa
Political Boundary

LIBYA

Al Aweinat
Jebel al-Uweinat (2000m)

LIBYAN DESERT

NUBIAN DESERT

Abri
Soleb Wawa

NORTHERN SUDAN

Kerma
Abu Hamed
Port Sudan
Suakin

Nukheila Oasis
Dongola
Kareima
Nuri
El-Kurru Merowe
Berber
Haiya

CHAD

Al-Atrun Oasis
Ed-Debba

NILE

Atbara
Karora

Sixth Cataract (Sabalooka Falls)
Begrawiya
Kabushiya
Shendi
Musawarat
Naga

KASSALA

Asmara

ERITREA

SUDAN

NORTHERN DARFUR

NORTHERN KORDOFAN

Omdurman
Bahri (Khartoum North)
KHARTOUM
Kassala
Teseney
Taka Mountains

EL-GEZIRA

Wad Medani
Shobak
Gedaref

WHITE NILE

El-Obeid
Kosti
Sennar
Dinder
Gallabat
Metema

Al-Geneina
El-Fasher

Jebel Marra (3088m)

An-Nahud
Dubeibat
Umm Ruwaba
Er-Rahad

Singa
BLUE NILE

Dinder National Park
Lake Tana
Gonder

Nyala
Al-Odaiya
Dilling
Ed-Damazin

SOUTHERN KORDOFAN

Nuba Mountains

Roseires Dam

SOUTHERN DARFUR

Birao
Am Dafog
Babanusa
Kadugli

SOBAT

Blue Nile

Malakal

BAHR AL-GHAZAL

Jur River
Sobat River

UPPER NILE

ETHIOPIA

Wau
AL-BOHAYRAT
The Sudd
JONGLEI

CENTRAL AFRICAN REPUBLIC

SOUTH SUDAN

Rumbek
Bor

Tambura

WESTERN EQUATORIA

White Nile

EASTERN EQUATORIA

Ilemi Triangle (Area of Dispute)

Doruma
Yambio
JUBA
Tonj
Kapoeta

Yei
Lokichoggio
Dongatona Mountains

Aba
Nimule
Immatong Mountains

DEMOCRATIC REPUBLIC OF CONGO

UGANDA

KENYA

Chapter Twelve

HOME AGAIN

Minneapolis 2009–12

I was in Juba, Southern Sudan, when I decided that I finally had had enough. The temperature rarely fell below 104 degrees Fahrenheit. I bathed in water pulled directly out of the Nile River, resulting in a mysterious growth on the side of my face. My house was infested with bats. Each night for weeks, the "eek, eek, eek" and fluttering of inverted wings squeaked through a small opening directly over my bed.

I came home one night to find a bat hanging lazily inside the netting that surrounded my bed. I went outside, ordering the two young men repairing my fence in the yard to assist me. Inside of the house, we tore up a cardboard box and positioned a chair under the opening to the rafters. Taking turns, the young men spotted each other as they tightly nailed the opening shut.

Yet, all of these discomforts were manageable. Something deeper and more personal had taken hold of me. A year had passed since the death of my friend. When I thought of the ambush, it haunted me as I visualized the white Land Cruiser riddled with bullet holes.

I thought back to the time that I had spent in Rwanda. Thirteen years had passed since I had climbed into my first white Land Cruiser. How many more years was I willing to take such incredible risks? For how much longer would luck continue to be my best friend out on the road? When would the inner peace that I so desperately sought cease to elude me? I needed to stop running. It was time to go home.

For the third time in my international career, I returned to the US. I rented an apartment in the same building in downtown Minneapolis, where I had lived seven years earlier. But instead of overlooking the Basilica, I opted for an apartment on the nineteenth floor with a magnificent view of the Minneapolis skyline. The Foshay Tower, the highest building in the city when I was a child, was nestled neatly outside of my window among a multitude of glass-plated hi-rise buildings.

I continued to travel overseas on short-term assignments as I had done twice before. Six months after arriving back in the US, I landed a consulting job in Darfur. It was Ramadan. I traveled with the field site director to Nyala in South Darfur. The security situation was tenuous following the abduction of an international humanitarian aid worker three months earlier.

I attended a dinner benefit in Khartoum before traveling to Nyala. The international community, along with their Sudanese colleagues and government partners, broke fast at sundown together in respect of the religious holiday. A communal prayer was offered with wishes for the abducted woman's immediate release. A jar was set out on a table with stacks of cut paper and piles of pencils for friends and colleagues to write messages to be delivered to the young woman when she was freed.

The first day I was in Nyala, I attended a meeting in the auditorium of the governor's office. The purpose of the meeting was to discuss rebel activity in the surrounding area. Humanitarian organizations could not access their areas of operation due to insecurity. Health clinics and community development programs, to support the internally displaced populations, were managed remotely. Expatriates had not been out to field sites outside of Nyala for months.

A dozen humanitarian workers filed into the room, taking seats around the rectangular table spanning the length of the room. The comfortable leather chairs had high backs and working wheels. Six-foot-high industrial fans whizzed loudly from two corners of the expansive room. We chatted idly as we waited.

Thirty minutes later, a staff member from the governor's office came into the room. We sat up. He informed us that the governor had ordered us to come back for the meeting in two hours. The group gathered their notebooks, nodded at each other, and filed out of the room.

"Why do we have to come back?" I asked as we got up from the table to leave. "The convocation from the governor for this meeting came an hour before we left the office this morning."

"This is typical," my colleague said.

"Do we have time to go to the market to buy a watermelon?" I asked.

Watermelons were in season. Large piles were scattered on the ground or in the back of dilapidated pickup trucks along the main road.

"We can do that now," he said, "and still return in time for the meeting."

As we walked through the doorway, a group of men in white robes entered the auditorium, pulling large stacks of plastic chairs behind them.

We climbed into the small rental car. The driver was listening to a tape in the tape deck. The cadence of the chanting filled the interior of the car. Thick, white, fake fur covered the dashboard. A decorative tissue box was nestled into the fur.

White tissues popped out of the top. A string of wooden prayer beads dangled from the rearview mirror. A laminated prayer card hung next to them. When I had been picked up from the airport, the back space had been wide enough for my small suitcase and nothing else.

My colleague instructed the driver to bring us to the central market. As we drove through the gates, we entered an area the size of a football field. In the center of the open area, five different vendors stood idly next to high piles of watermelons that had been poured out of the back of truck beds. The area around the watermelon stands was barren—nothing else was for sale.

My colleague agreed to do my bidding. I passed him a note in local currency equivalent to five US dollars. He took the note and stepped out of the car. I was the only woman in the marketplace. Leaning back into the window, he told me to wait for him in the car. The driver turned off the ignition and joined my colleague in the center of the dusty field. They moved from pile to pile, picking up watermelons, haggling with the vendors. Although my colleague was African, he was not Sudanese. He stood slapping the hands of the vendors, launching jokes, needling them with compliments. As I watched, he selected a small, round melon. After pressing the bill into the vendor's palm, he shook his hand and returned to the car. As he opened the back door, he handed me the melon. It was warm. I placed it on the seat next to me.

We returned to the auditorium at the governor's office. Enough chairs had been placed throughout the auditorium to seat more than two hundred people. Most of the chairs were already filled. Men in white robes chatted with each other as the women sat quietly—methodically pulling their light, cotton cover-ups back over their heads, repositioning the cloth that had slipped out of place.

My colleague and I took two seats at the far end of the auditorium in the first row. I waved my notebook in front of my face, creating a slight breeze. We waited. A buzz of confusion permeated the room. Three men with video cameras were positioned at different angles throughout the room.

"They're going to release the woman who was abducted today," I whispered to my colleague.

"What?" he asked. "How do you know?"

"I don't," I said. "It's just a sense that I have."

Ten minutes later, the governor walked into the room with a young woman. She was small and slim. She looked as if she were wearing clean but borrowed clothes.

The governor opened the press conference.

There was one other woman from the international community in the room. She jumped up, walked briskly to the front of the room, and sat next to the young woman. It was the first time that anyone from the international community had seen her since the abduction.

My eyes filled immediately with tears. I looked down to mask them. One of the cameramen spotted my reaction and turned his camera on me. The Sudanese woman sitting next to me looked over at me and patted me on the knee.

"All is good. Praise God," she said in Arabic.

The young woman stood in front of the crowd as she gave a statement to thank the governor for his role in her release. Two of the cameramen moved in closer to the young woman. The third cameraman kept his camera pointed on me. The young woman's friend had joined her at the head table without an invitation from the governor. The friend leaned over and told the young woman that she didn't have to make any comments to the press. The governor—incensed—raised his arm and pointed toward the entrance, ordering the young woman's friend out of the room.

I kept my head down, trying to stop the shaking in my shoulders. I did not know the young American woman standing next to the governor, staring out into the crowd, but I was the only other American in the room. Her friend had been banished, she would be whisked away after the press conference, and no one would be allowed to speak with her.

Although I had not responded to her, the Sudanese woman sitting next to me continued to console me. The man with the video camera moved in closer. The words: "All is good," swirled around me in Arabic. But it was not—the young woman at the front of the auditorium had yet to be freed.

In Nyala, we were under lockdown from dusk to dawn. The office was less than a five-minute walk from the staff compound, but we were not allowed to be alone on the street at any time. The Ramadan celebration, marking the end of the religious month of fasting, lasted for three days. My Muslim colleagues spent this time feasting with their families. I remained in the guesthouse with the other international staff, drinking freeze-dried coffee and eating tuna from a can. I also had a watermelon. If we did not lose power during the night, it would be chilled by the following morning—in time for the holiday.

I researched travel options and caught up on personal affairs. I wrote to Paul. In the message, I referenced the photo that he had taken of my driver spinning out in the desert four years earlier. I asked him for permission to use the photo on the cover of my book. Within minutes, he rang me on my local cell in Sudan. "Julie, this is Paul," he said.

"Hey, hi," I said.

He was calling from a location outside of Brussels. He was going into the compound where he and his colleagues conducted training courses. He only had a few minutes to talk.

"How long have you been in Nyala?" he asked.

"I got here on Thursday."

"How did you fly in?"

I told him that I had flown in on the UN flight from Khartoum.

"I flew out on the UN flight on Thursday."

"Wow," I said. "I was traveling with a colleague who went back to the plane to look for his bag. If I had gone with him, I would have seen you on the tarmac."

I couldn't believe that I had been standing in the arrivals lounge of the small airport as Paul was preparing to depart from the room next to me.

"I'm with the guys," he said. "I told them that you are there."

The second comment lingered—I didn't know the guys. I had known Paul for many years. He had done pro-bono work for me in central Africa, so I understood that his colleagues may have known about me. I was touched, however, that he may have mentioned me to them at other times as well.

His car was approaching the entrance to the training compound. He needed to shut off his phone. His voice quickened. He still had the phone message I had left for him the day my friend had been killed in Afghanistan, and he had recently replayed it. He had saved the message as a *wav* audio file. I told him that I had been so distraught when I had left the message that I had not remembered what I had said to him that night. He needed to go. He said that he would send me the file.

I returned to Rwanda. It had been fifteen years since my departure. I had never wanted to return to Kigali, fearing that painful memories would come back to haunt me if I did. Upon landing, however, instead of being traumatized, I marveled at the advancements that the government had made since the genocide. There was wide-spread construction. Where land-mines had been cleared, modern buildings had been erected. The government was working to build the tourism industry. While neighboring countries had health issues resulting from refuge strewn in open gutters along the streets, Rwanda was remarkably clean. There were no thin, plastic bags hanging off of withered tree branches—they had been outlawed.

Amid the advancements, however, I was painfully aware that trauma and human rights abuses simmered under the surface, threatening to boil over. No matter how pristine the city may have become, an incredible amount of work remained to be done before the country could boast a well-functioning civil society.

I also returned to Southern Sudan. I had not been to Juba since I left my previous organization more than two years earlier. I had hired a new country director, and I needed to travel to Juba to provide training and orientation for her. Senada was new to the organization. I was pleased that she had accepted the position; her commitment to Southern Sudan was solid—she had worked in Juba some years earlier, and she had wanted to return to support the transition.

Originally from Bosnia, she understood well what was needed to build a newly independent state. Southern Sudan had held a referendum in July 2011. After the votes were counted, a new name was adopted and The Republic of South Sudan became the newest country in Africa—boosting the number of independent countries on the continent from fifty-three to fifty-four.

Prior to the referendum, there had been two levels of conflict. At the national level, there were tensions between

Muslims in the north and Animists in the south. Oil lingered under borders that were in the south. Many of these borders were fiercely disputed by the government in the north.

Although independence was granted for the south, after the referendum, regional conflicts between pastoral tribes, which had been raging for centuries did not allow for an immediate peace. The tribal conflicts that had led to insecurity in the country continued to threaten communities and travelers passing through the areas. During my site visit with the country director, I would find myself on the same road that had caused me concern two years earlier.

When we arrived at the office, the security officer briefed the country director. There had been reports of tribal clashes on the road. Two vehicles traveling from Juba had been turned back. A string of commercial trucks were awaiting clearance to cross the border. The departure time was pushed back and the team traveling was put on standby until the security issues in the area were resolved. Two hours later, we were provided with an update. A vehicle had gained passage through the corridor. Commercial trucks had been allowed to pass through customs at the border. An hour later, the team I had been waiting to travel with was cleared to depart.

It was mid-day at one, and the field site was just over four hours away. For security reasons, we were not allowed to travel by road outside of Juba after dark; it would be necessary to arrive before nightfall. Four staff climbed into the vehicle. The country director sat in the front seat with the driver. I was in the back with another colleague. The white Land Cruiser was a newer model than I had traveled in before—it had functioning air conditioning.

As we neared the area on the road that had been insecure earlier that day, we spotted smoke. Small fires along the side of the road were commonplace throughout the country. Refuse was regularly collected, dumped into the street, and burned. But the smoke billowing along the side of the road was thicker than usual. Young men, armed with machetes and homemade spears, ran along the road in front of us. The country director instructed the driver to slow down. We inched past the fire.

A man was lying on the side of the road—facedown. A woman was crawling away from the man, edging her way back toward the small shop that had been pillaged and burned. A white flour-like substance had been flung along the ground in front of the shop. Few people remained at the scene. Women and children were fleeing along the road, stumbling as they looked back in fear.

As we drove on, the road ahead of us was deserted. We came upon a pickup truck. An automatic rifle was attached to the top of the cab of the truck. Two men were standing in the truck bed—government soldiers, patrolling the area to stabilize the instability between the warring tribes.

The country director waved at the soldiers in greeting. The soldiers waved back, slowing to allow our vehicle to pass. We entered the center of a small town, the open lot on the side of the road a transit point used by international organizations as a kiss point. In order not to travel by night, international organizations often sent two vehicles from diametric locations to meet at a central point on the road. Once at the kiss point, drivers remained with the vehicles while passengers, cargo, and luggage were exchanged.

I thought of my friend who had been traveling in a convoy in Afghanistan two years earlier. She had been on her way to a kiss point, but her vehicle was ambushed by the Taliban before she had arrived. I had known and worked with her in three countries over the years, and I was still grieving her loss. I thought of three other humanitarian workers who had been slain in Somalia earlier that year.

Even though I had returned home and was based in Minneapolis, I was increasingly finding myself in some of the most dangerous countries in the world. The year before, I had traveled to Somalia, Pakistan, and Darfur, a state in the west of Sudan, during periods of heightened insecurity. While I was in these countries, abductions and ambushes had been commonplace.

For years, my aunt had cautioned me about going into countries where there were risks due to conflict. She continually had pleaded with me to give up my international work and find a job in the US. I called her after I had settled back in Minneapolis. She was pleased to learn that I had landed a job as an executive in the US. But, due to the nature of my work, I found myself back on that road.

We passed the kiss point. We were staying overnight, so we had not needed to arrange for a driver from the field site to meet us there. Rain clouds were amassing in the sky ahead of us. By the time we reached the field site, it would be raining.

We rounded a bend in the road. A pile of logs had been stacked in the middle of the road to create a makeshift roadblock. The country director told the driver to stop. We watched as a group of young men surrounded the car ahead of us on the road. We had enough time and space to turn around, but as the car in front of us accelerated through the roadblock, the driver of our vehicle also accelerated, pulling us into the middle of the group of young, armed men.

We were immediately surrounded. Young men and boys, three deep on each side of the vehicle, were yelling and shaking spears. I turned around to see a large truck pull up behind us, blocking us in.

The youth pelted the windows with thick slabs of rubber. A tire iron struck the window above my passenger door. I pulled my head away from the window as it was struck again.

"They're smashing, they're smashing," I repeated senselessly.

Three windows were down. The two doors on the left side of the vehicle were open. Earlier, as we had passed the burning shop, we had ensured that all of the locks in the vehicle were secured. The driver was pleading with the youth, assuring them that he was not a member of the tribe that the youth were seeking for retribution. The male colleague to my left was African. He told the youth he was from a neighboring country. He was not Southern Sudanese.

I looked over at my passenger door. The lock was up. I reached over and punched it back down. Out of the corner of my eye, I saw two youths circle around to the back of the vehicle. I turned to look—the back door was open. In all of my years overseas, I had never been in a Land Cruiser that did not have manual locks for the back door. I wondered if the youth had tripped the lock with their arrows. Two young men stood in front of the open door. I glimpsed the expression on the face of the young man closest to the door. It had yet to register in his mind to reach his hand forward and pull the backpack lying in front of him out of the truck.

I turned and dove, reaching for the back of the truck in one fell swoop. As I pulled the door shut, I cautioned myself not to catch the hands of the young man standing in front of the door.

I heard a shriek.

"What's that?!"

My long skirt had flown up over my waist as I dove over the backseat. My rear end was exposed. The country director reached over and pulled my skirt back down over my legs. I teetered on the back of the seat, staring at the lock on the back door. My body hung in mid-air, stretched along the length of the back of the truck. The lock held.

I slipped back into my seat and looked over at the passenger door beside me—it was still locked. The other passengers continued to plead and negotiate with the hysterical youth yelling outside of their open doors and windows. I turned my head to check the door at the rear of the vehicle. It was still secured. I made eye contact with a young boy standing at the back of the truck. Through the back window, he pointed at me, held his hand up to his throat, and made a slicing motion. I held his gaze, slowly shaking my head from side to side. He nodded affirmatively, pointed at me again, and made the same slicing motion. I continued to hold his gaze as I slowly shook my head for a second time. He was a child. As he threatened my life, I stared calmly into his eyes.

The pickup truck with the government soldiers that we had passed along the road earlier approached our vehicle from the side. "Tell your driver to go! Tell your driver to go!" one of the soldiers screamed at the country director through her open window.

She yelled at the driver, "Go! Go!"

The driver pulled his passenger door shut and accelerated, releasing the vehicle from the roadblock. The large truck behind us advanced. As the government soldiers pulled their pickup truck over to the side of the road, the youth dispersed. The driver pulled his cell phone out of his pocket.

"John, stop! John, stop! Pull over!" the country director screamed.

He kept driving, fumbling with his cell phone.

"John," I cried from the backseat, "what are you doing?

"John," yelled the country director again. "Stop!"

The driver pulled over as he continued to fumble with his cell phone.

"John," I screamed again, "what are you doing?"

"I'm going to call the police," he said.

I sat back, relieved to be out of the roadblock. Police reform had begun with the support of the international community in Juba, but there was a very limited, and often absent, police presence outside of the capital.

The country director asked the driver if he was all right. He nodded that he was fine. The colleague sitting next to me in the backseat told the country director that he was also fine. The country director twisted around in her seat to look back at me.

"Are you okay?" she asked.

"Yeah," I said. "I'm fine, you?"

"I still have my Mac," she said.

The driver slipped his phone back into his pocket, and we drove off—our collective shock strapping us in behind our seat belts. For a long time, we were all quiet. Outside, we were the only vehicle on the road.

When we arrived at the field site, it was raining. I opened the door and looked for a smooth area on the ground without puddles. As I stretched my leg out of the vehicle and placed my foot on the ground, a sharp pain shot up my leg—I had broken a toe. I looked down. The skin on my foot reflected the light in a soft pink glow. By nightfall, my foot would take on a blue-black hue.

I pulled my foot behind me as we entered the compound. I continued to pull my foot behind me as I visited the departments in the field site, all housed in *tukels* constructed on a wide, open yard. I kept my movements to a minimum that evening, choosing not to walk across the yard to fetch warm water for my bucket shower.

Sam called. I had not heard from him in weeks. I had met him in Liberia, where I had lived a year earlier during a four-month consulting job.

"How are you?" he asked.

"Hang on," I said.

I set down my laptop, stood up, and pulled my foot out of the communal *tukel* where I was sitting with my colleagues. I walked away from the thatched structure, dragging my foot behind me until I found a place in the open yard where I could talk privately.

"Hi," I said. "I'm fine. But Sam," I took a breath, "something happened."

"What happened, baby?" he asked.

"I broke my toe at a roadblock," I said.

"Ohhhhhhhhh, so sorry," he said.

Whenever he called, he asked about my parents. Then he asked me to greet them on his behalf. He had a three-year-old daughter who lived with him. His mother, a Liberian, was living in the US after having left her own country at the start of the civil war. Sam had been taken back to Lebanon with his father as a small child, and he had not seen his mother since he was three years old.

As I traveled back and forth to Liberia, I carried photos to each of them from the other. During these visits, I saw firsthand how much they both had suffered as a result of their long separation.

Through my friendship with Sam, I learned what I needed to do to improve the quality of my own life. My relationship with my mother had been strained for years. And, while Sam was unable to see or spend time with his mother, I could easily arrange to see and spend time with mine.

"Sam," I said, "thank you so much for calling. I really needed to hear your voice today. You are my angel."

"It's okay," he said sheepishly.

I didn't want him to use all of his prepaid phone credits.

"I have to go now. Say 'hi' to the baby for me. Give her a big hug and a kiss," I said.

"I will," he said. "Don't work too hard."

"I won't," I said. "Bye, *Habibi*."

The next day we returned to Juba by a different route. We crossed the border, stamped our passports, and took a boat, straddling two countries to a location near another field site back in the new Republic of South Sudan. We were met by the field coordinator, an impressive young woman who put us up in her small house. We stopped for dinner at a local restaurant. We bought beer at the only bar in town. After depositing our luggage in our rooms, we met outside on the terrace, snapped the bottle caps off of the large, dark bottles of warm beer, and drank it under the stars.

Prior to departing for South Sudan, I had met with my supervisor to inform him that I would be leaving the organization upon my return. During my trip, I had reconsidered my decision. After the day that I put my overnight bag into the back of the white Land Cruiser, however, remaining with the organization was no longer an option.

Before securing the lock on my passenger door that day, I had had a thought that was surprisingly free of expletives. Petrified, I had thought: *This can go horribly wrong.* Three months later, the fear that had frozen inside of me that day resurfaced. I made an appointment with Jim Moore to work through the post-traumatic shock. Working with Jim had helped me. But for a year afterward, if I looked over and saw that the passenger door on the right side of the car was unlocked while I was driving, I quickly pressed the automatic lock button. It was only then that I could breathe easily.

For years, I had stretched my luck to the limit. Back in Minneapolis, I resigned my position at the small international nonprofit where I had been working to focus more seriously on my writing. I completed the manuscript that I had been working on for over two years. After more than seven years, I began writing sonnets again.

My search for inner peace had come to an end. By increasing the stillness in the space around me, I found what I had sought over a lifetime. The clarity and volume of my inner voice increased. No longer were crackly sound waves—reminiscent of the scratchy and unintelligible VHF radio transmissions between the base in the countries where I had worked and the white Land Cruisers out on the road—informing my life. I was listening more intently to myself.

Today, each night as I unfurl the blinds, I watch as the Minneapolis skyline dissolves in front of me. Each morning when I awake, I stand at the window, shielding my eyes as the sunlight streams into the room around me. There are times, however, when I am not in Minneapolis—I still travel. Yet, no matter where I am in the world, I do not need to look far to find that I am home. Borders are invisible barriers, when your soul is alive and your heart is at peace.

AFTER THE CONFLICT, BEFORE THE PEACE

After the conflict, before the peace, tell
Me—what is left of life when a beating heart
Is cut out of a chest—cleaving? Ripping
Back flesh, warm blood on your hands—eternal
Life or unsung death? At once you take flight,
Waning on a river, winding freely
Through deep-cut channels until, squinting—
You find yourself deposited safely
On the other side. Oh! The cool waters,
Warm sun waxing, spring emerges, marking
Time on the smoothest of stones—hard as nails,
Your soul once again filled with life. Without
Question you pick yourself up, content in
Knowing, this day—that, yes!—you are alive.

Minneapolis, Minnesota, 2012

ITALY

0 ___ 100 km
0 ___ 60 miles

FRANCE
GERMANY
Munich
VIENNA
SLOVAKIA
Basel
Zurich
VADUZ
BUDAPEST
Lucerne
LIECHTENSTEIN
Innsbruck
AUSTRIA
BERN
SWITZERLAND
Val Gardena
HUNGARY
Bolzano
Dobbiaco
Cortina d'Ampezzo
SERBIA
Mont Blanc (4807m)
Courmayeur
San Martino di Castrozza
Canazei
Aosta
VALLE D'AOSTA
Verbania
Sondrio
TRENTINO-ALTO ADIGE
Belluno
FRIULI-VENEZIA GIULIA
SLOVENIA
LJUBLJANA
ZAGREB
Bassano
Bergamo
Trent
Treviso
Trieste
Karlovac
CROATIA
Turin
Milan
LOMBARDY
Brescia
Verona
Vicenza
Padua
VENETO
Venice
Gulf of Venezia
Rijeka
PIEDMONT
Monviso (3841m)
Alessandria
Piacenza
Mantua
Bania Luka
Cuneo
LIGURIA
Genoa
EMILIA-ROMAGNA
Parma
Modena
Ferrara
BOSNIA HERZEGOVINA
Savona
Santa Margherita
Bologna
Ravenna
Zadar
Imperia
Gulf of Genova
La Spezia
Cesena
Rimini
SARAJEVO
Nice
Parco Nazionale delle Cinque Terre
Lucca
Pistoia
Forlì
Pesaro
Urbino
MONACO
Pisa
Florence
SAN MARINO
Ancona
Split
LIGURIAN SEA
Livorno
TUSCANY
Arezzo
Gubbio
LE MARCHE
Capraia
San Gimignano
Siena
Perugia
Assisi
MONTENEGRO
Piombino
Pienza
UMBRIA
Dubrovnik
Bastia
Elba
Montepulciano
Grosseto
Spoleto
CORSICA (Fr)
Viterbo
Tarquinia
LAZIO
L'Aquila
Pescara
ADRIATIC SEA
Civitavecchia
Cerveteri
Chieti
Fiumicino
ROME
Tivoli
ABRUZZO
Parco Nazionale del Gargano
Promontorio del Gargano
Ostia Antica
Frosinone
MOLISE
Latina
Campobasso
Foggia
Gulf of Gaeta
Mt CAMPANIA Vesuvius (1277m)
Benevento
Caserta
Andria
Bari
PUGLIA
Asinara
Naples
Avellino
Potenza
Matera
Brindisi
Porto Torres
Olbia
Golfo Aranci
Sassari
Ischia
Pompei
Salerno
BASILICATA
Taranto
Lecce
Alghero
Sorrento
Capri
Paestum
Otranto
Bosa
Nuoro
Dorgali
Gulf of Orosei
Amalfi Coast
Gulf of Taranto
Gallipoli
Oristano
Cala Gonone
TYRRHENIAN SEA
Arbatax
CALABRIA
SARDINIA
Cosenza
Cagliari
Catanzaro
Crotone
Capo Rizzuto
Sant'Antioco
AEOLIAN ISLANDS
Salina
Stromboli
Gulf of Squillace
IONIAN SEA
Filicudi
Panarea
Alicudi
Lipari
Vulcano
Milazzo
Messina
Trapani
Palermo
Mt Etna (3320m)
Reggio di Calabria
Marsala
Cefalù
Taormina
MEDITERRANEAN SEA
Catania
Agrigento
SICILY
Syracuse
Ragusa
Pozzallo
Pantelleria
ALGERIA
TUNIS
TUNISIA
VALLETTA
MALTA

Epilogue

REVELATIONS, REVEALED

Rome 2012

Carmen was sitting alone. A hard-sided, medium-sized pink suitcase, with anatomic wheels, steeled her against pedestrians. Passersby slipped onto the street to dodge her makeshift office space. A truncated canvas stool served as a table for her readings. A second canvas stool elevated her knees. White moon boots, the color of her hair, stood higher than her thighs as she sat. Her bright pink lipstick, the same shade as her suitcase, was smudged.

I stopped on the street in front of her.

"*Quanto?*" How much, I asked.

She looked me up and down.

"Ten euro," she said.

I told her that I would give her seven. She waved me lower. I sat on the cement curb in front of her, pulling my skirt over my legs, leaving my ankles exposed out in the street. Carmen smoothed a deck of tarot cards onto the small canvas table in front of her.

"Choose ten," she instructed.

Her eyes darted from side to side. I perused the deck splayed out on the canvas table in front of me, leisurely pulling out ten cards.

"Are you looking for someone?" I asked.

Ignoring me, her eyes continued to dart from side to side. I handed the ten cards that I had selected from the pile across the table, wondering if she had been shooed away by the authorities on previous nights.

"Five more," she said, pointing at the pile of overturned cards between us.

I chose five more cards and handed them to her. She laid out the cards, lining them out in three rows, each row cascading one over the other. She pointed at a card along the bottom row closest to her.

"There is a man in your past," she said.

I looked over at her, amazed by her deep insight.

"He loves you," she said.

She looked across the table at me.

"Do you love him?"

I gazed back at her, thinking of someone.

"Uh, yes, I do," I said.

"*In tre mesi,*" she said, holding up three fingers.

Turning the card toward me, she pointed at it again, pushing it into the canvas tabletop.

"You will be together *in tre mesi.*"

She scooped up the cards and slipped them facedown on the top of the pink suitcase beside her. She handed me the remaining deck. Her eyes resumed their darting dance. She told me to choose ten more cards. I plucked ten cards out of the deck that she had handed me. She looked back at me, nodding toward the deck. I plucked out five more.

I wondered which ghost from my past would appear to sweep me off of my feet. I considered a few options as I pulled out the cards. None seemed viable. I handed her the cards. She positioned them in three rows. Her eyes popped over the cards as she pondered their meaning. She slipped a card out of the middle row.

"You will have much money," she said.

Good, I thought, my savings would quickly be running out. I had loved the work that I had been doing in Minneapolis, but I had not liked the job. A month earlier, I had left my position to pursue my writing.

Her eyes rolled over the rows of cards. She looked back up at the top row, running through each card from top to bottom a second time.

"I don't see any work," she said. "What is your work?"

"I don't have any work right now," I replied.

"Mhmmph," she grunted.

She gathered up the cards, slipping them on the used pile with one hand, smoothing out the remaining cards on the top of the makeshift table with the other.

"*Ancora*," again, she ordered.

What next? I wondered.

Shifting on the cement curb, I was careful not to snag the soft material of my skirt. For the first time since I had sat down, Carmen seemed relaxed. I quickly pulled out ten cards and handed them to her. I pulled out five more. As she laid out the cards, I asked her where she was from.

"The south," she said. "Calabria."

I understood why she was looking around furtively. Italians from the south were frowned upon in the north. The resentment, no doubt resulting from the criminal syndicates that originated in Italy in the mid-nineteenth century. Maximilian—Max—the taxi driver who had driven me from my hotel in Radda in Chianti to the Florence airport, had tutored me on the various syndicates during the long ride. He had told me that the north of Italy had financially supported the south for decades.

During our discussion, Max had listed the most prominent criminal syndicates in the country: the Camorra from Naples in Campania; the *Sacra Conona Unita*, or Holy Crown, of Puglia in Apulia; and the *Cosa Nostra*, or Mafia of Sicily. He had said that there were also others.

"The Mafia is the most well-known of the syndicates," he said. "But the word mafia is overused. As I say, there are more—the *'Ndrangheta* of Calabria is now the most powerful syndicate in the south."

"That's interesting," I said. "How do you spell that?"

I took out a notepad and wrote down the various syndicates that he had mentioned. He quickly glanced over at the notepad that I held up. He spelled out *'Ndrangheta* as he looked out at the road in front of him.

"I'm American, but my family originated from Calabria."

He looked over at me.

"No problem," he said. "But believe me—I am telling you—this is our history.

"What's the difference between the north and the south in Italy?" I asked.

"Look around you, Tuscany is so beautiful. We have organic products. You cannot find the same in the south," he said. "We have standards. In the south, they have a code."

Being from Calabria, I expected that Carmen was not entirely welcome in the capital city of her own country. Yet, to me, she embodied my heritage. I felt an immediate kinship with her.

"My mother's family is from Calabria," I said, looking across the table at Carmen. "We are *Calabresi.*"

She looked up from the cards.

"You," I said, pointing at her. "Me," I said, pointing back at myself.

She smiled. "*Calabresi*, you and me," she snorted, shaking her head. "We are *Calabresi.*"

The conversation was taxing our limited vocabulary. She looked down at the cards.

"I see a woman, a new friend," she began.

Her fingers were back to pointing at the cards. She turned one over and pushed it toward me.

"This new friend, she will betray you," she said, tapping the top of the card as she looked at me.

I stared back at her.

One night there had been a party. My best friend and my boyfriend had had the night off. As I reached into the bin to grab fresh silverware to set up my tables at the end of the night, a chill had run down my spine as I had thought, *They are together*—a premonition confirmed the next day. I wondered what betrayal would be like as an adult, knowing what I now knew—that we rarely say or do things with the intention of hurting others, using our words and actions instead as shields.

I looked over at Carmen. She was preparing to leave. I pulled out a ten-euro note. Carmen said that she didn't have change, but that she could break the note at the gelato shop across the street. I turned and looked. On the other side of the street was the façade of a church.

Carmen stood up as she packed her things. If I raised my arm, she could stand comfortably under it.

"I'll go with you," I said. "I'd like to buy you a gelato."

She folded the short, steel bars of her canvas table and slipped it into her suitcase. She folded the stool, slipped it on top of the table and snapped the suitcase shut.

When we reached the gelato shop, the blue eye shadow above her dark eyes peeled back into her lids as she stood in front of the glass case. She looked up at me gleefully, and I told her she could have whatever she wanted. She ordered a strawberry gelato with whipped cream. She asked me if I wanted whipped cream on mine.

"I'll just have the mint," I said, looking up at the young man behind the glass case.

"One scoop or two?" he asked.

"Two for her and one for me," I replied.

I paid for the gelato with a twenty-euro note. From the change, I pulled out a five-euro note and two ones. I folded the notes and handed them to Carmen. She skimmed a spoonful of the soft whipped cream off of the top of her gelato, slipped it into her mouth, and pushed the cup into my hand. She rifled through her large handbag. A coin purse emerged in her hand, she pulled it open—it was empty. Snapping it shut, she took the bills out of my hand and asked me to wait while she went into the restroom. When she came out, I handed her the cup of gelato.

"*Grazie,*" thank you, she said, looking up at me. Her eyes grew large, "*Mamma Mia!*"

She thrust the cup back into my hand and spun around, her moon boots gliding on the floor as she made her way back to the restroom. When she returned, she was clutching the euro notes that I had given her between her fingers.

She stood beside me, head down, intently eating her gelato. When she was finished, I looked up at the clock on the wall of the shop. It was ten at night.

"Where are you going now?" I asked.

She was going to catch a bus from the *Piazza Venezia*. Halfway to the *piazza* was my hotel, on the same street where Carmen had given me the reading. I told her that I would walk her to the square.

"Is the Plaza your hotel?" she asked.

I told her that I was staying in the area.

She looked up at me knowingly. Reaching into her handbag, she asked me for my phone number. She pulled out a small notebook, and I wrote my name and number on the open page that she had pushed toward me.

"I will call you when I am back in Calabria," she said.

Carmen and I had became fast friends—the bedrock of nomads. I welcomed her company—I had been traveling alone for a month. As we passed my hotel, she looked up, but I didn't stop. Together, we walked on. I asked her if she would like to speak to my mother.

"*Si, si, perché no?*" Yes, yes, why not, she replied.

Growing up, my mother lived with her immigrant grandparents in Minneapolis. Newly married, her grandfather had left the south of Italy for the US, arriving at Ellis Island alone. His young wife, who had not wanted to leave her home in Calabria, had stayed behind with their infant son. Seven years later, my great-grandmother joined my great-grandfather in Minneapolis. Due to an illness, their first-born son had been turned away at the docks in Italy, and he would not be reunited with his parents until he was a young man.

The light changed, and we crossed the street. I pulled out my iPhone, searching the contact list for *Mom and Pop*. I pulled the screen down with my finger and tapped the contact. It connected. My mother answered, and I said hello.

"I'm here with Carmen," I said. "She's from Calabria and she wants to talk to you."

I thrust the phone toward Carmen. She took it from my hand and pulled it to her ear.

"*Buona sera, come sta?*" Good evening, how are you, she asked.

She was silent for a moment.

"*Io sono Carmen,*" I am Carmen, she said. There was a pause. "Carmen," she said again. "I am with your daughter."

She poked the air in front of me with her finger.

"Julie," I whispered down to her.

"Julie," she repeated into the phone. "I give her reading, very good, reading very good."

Yeah, I thought, the "you will have a lot of money" part, wishing I could welcome the old lover and skirt the betrayal.

"Calabria," Carmen said. She pushed the phone back at me. "She no understand."

I took the phone.

"I need to go, Mom," I said. "I'm going to walk Carmen to the square to catch her bus."

I looked down at Carmen.

"Mom, you'd love her. She looks just like your grandmother!"

I hung up the phone, and without looking, slipped it into my bag. Carmen and I continued walking in silence. I thought of my mother, happy to be close to her again. For many years, we had had struggles. Yet, when I had needed to, I had pulled from her strength—no matter where I had been in the world.

I stopped as we neared the square.

"It was so nice to meet you, Carmen," I said. "Thank you for talking to my mother. She was very happy to talk to you."

Carmen's eyes grew bright.

I leaned over. "Good-bye," I said as I hugged her.

She told me again that she would call me. Although I did not expect to hear from her, my name was written in her notebook, and she would carry it with her when she traveled back to Calabria.

I watched as she walked away, her pink suitcase gliding waist-high beside her. After a few steps, she stopped and looked back.

"Ciao!" I said, waving.

Carmen smiled, and without speaking, she turned and rolled away.

A few blocks from my hotel, I ducked into a side street to call my mother, but the call did not go through. As I slipped the phone back into the interior pocket of my bag, I saw the euro notes that I had intended to give to Carmen as a gift.

I turned back toward the square, walking as quickly as possible, hoping to find her before she boarded her bus. When I reached the square, traffic loomed from every angle. I kept my eyes low, searching for a pink suitcase, white moon boots—a head of white hair. I crossed the square. Dozens of people were lined up at bus stops along side streets. Buses pulled up, stopped, and drove off—dark puffs of smoke billowing in their wake. Squinting through the exhaust, I circled the entire square.

I turned onto *Via del Corso,* toward my hotel. Carmen's white hair, white moon boots—the anatomic wheels attached to her suitcase—had eluded me. The delight upon her face, however, as she stood in anticipation of a cup of strawberry gelato, had been etched into my mind forever.

I stopped and looked up at the moon. Carmen was somewhere nearby under the same moon. I thought of the many other fast friends who had passed through my life over the years. By gazing up at the moon, I had managed to remain connected to them all.

I approached the corner where Carmen and I had spoken to my mother. As I waited for the light to change, I smiled and shook my head as I remembered our brief time together. "*Noi siamo Calabresi,* you and me," I said aloud. "Carmen, *noi siamo Calabresi.*"

AUTHOR'S NOTE

The question that so many people ask me when I return from overseas is: *What was it like?* The first time that I was asked this question, I was newly returned from Morocco, and it was a struggle to sum up over three years of my life in one sound bite. More than twenty-five years later, I will attempt to sum up my experiences in one page.

Readjustment became easier. I found that I could slide comfortably between cultures when I stopped wanting the place where I was to be someplace different. I learned that if I focused on the unique aspects of each place, I didn't pine after what I did not, or could not, have.

There were times while I was away when I pushed myself too hard. I paid for my experiences with exhaustion and illness, including malaria more than once. I paid for my experiences with splintered, disjointed relationships. But I did not pay for my experiences in sorrow.

I have gained so much from my international travels. The lessons have been many, but the themes have been few. Through my travels, I learned that people want a better life for themselves and their children. They want to feel safe and secure. They want to live their lives with respect and dignity. But most importantly, people want to be loved. The people I have met around the world have taught me that— notwithstanding our many cultural differences—at our very core, we are all the same.

ABOUT THE AUTHOR

Julie R. Dargis is based in Minneapolis, Minnesota. In addition to writing poetry and essays, she has worked as a country director and a management consultant, providing assistance to communities affected by conflict and natural disasters in Africa, Asia, Eastern Europe and the Caribbean. She began writing sonnets when she was a Peace Corps volunteer in Morocco. She publishes her work though Indie House Press, an independent imprint. She also manages a website to promote her work as well as the work of others. To learn more, visit: www. IndieHousePress.org.

HAVE YOU BEEN AFFECTED IN SOME WAY BY THIS BOOK?

Recount and post similar stories from your own life living and working overseas at www.PitStopintheParisofAfrica.tumblr. com.

To post a review, visit the author's page on GoodReads.com or the Amazon.com page for *Pit Stop in the Paris of Africa*.

Look for *Pit Stop in the Paris of Africa* on e-books.
Audio version and book app coming soon.